John and Pat Underwood

walk & eat
MADEIRA

CONTENTS

This pocket guide is designed for short-break walking holidays on Madeira, using public transport (or a car, if you prefer). Funchal, the capital, is easily and fairly inexpensively reached by charter flights, and the climate makes for brilliant walking all year round.

Fly out for just a week. You have in your hand enough walks, excursions, restaurants and recipes to last two weeks — so you can pick and choose the most appealing.

The highlights at a glance:

- 13 varied day walks, each with topographical map
- 2 excursions — one just a short 'flight' by cable car, the other a fairly long bus ride, with walks from each
- recommended restaurants and hotels
- recipes to make at your self-catering base or back home
- special section with hints on wheat-, gluten- and dairy-free eating and cooking on the island

INTRO

THE WALKS

The walks in this book (a 'baker's dozen') range from easy, flat routes along *levadas* (irrigation channels) to moderate hillside hikes. Dotted round the island (see map on pages 126-127), they have been chosen because they are *easily reached by bus and there is good eating en route.* For a very wide selecion of island walks, we recommend *Landscapes of Madeira,* with over 100 different routes. Now in its eighth edition, the book has been the 'walkers' Bible' for 25 years and was the first of Sunflower's 'Landscapes' guides. This series now covers 45 destinations. For more information see www.sunflowerbooks.co.uk.

THE EXCURSIONS

Two 'days out' are described. The first is just a short cable car ride to the hills above Funchal, where you can visit some lovely gardens and have lunch. It's an outing in itself, but also the jumping-off point for Walks 1 and 2. The second excursion, much beloved of users of *Landscapes of Madeira,* is a bus trip that takes in the north and west of the island. A four-hour stop for lunch at Porto Moniz allows you plenty of time to swim in the attractive lido — preferably *after* doing Walk 13.

THE RESTAURANTS

We have *featured* the restaurants (and hotels) we use regularly and say why we like them. In each case we include a 'mini-menu' listing some of their specialities. A price guide is given (€ to €€€) to indicate 'very reasonable' to 'fairly pricey'. But remember that you can have a relatively inexpensive meal in a five-star hotel if you just have a light lunch — for instance soup or an omelette. Our lunch at the Quinta do Furão, for example (two soups, one platter of grilled limpets shared between two and a full bottle of wine) cost just 24 €. The atmosphere was delightful, and they also served a huge tray of free 'nibbles' while we waited.

No restaurant has paid — in cash or in kind — to be included in this guide.

> If you would like to know more about Madeiran recipes, look out for a book called *Secrets of Madeira Cooking* by Zita Cardoso (available in most souvenir shops). Delia Smith has no competition here; the 'secrets' remain secret (some ingredients are missing and there are no oven temperatures or cooking times, *but* the book is fascinating nevertheless, with a huge variety of recipes — an unending source of inspiration! While it was written in cooperation with the Madeira Hotel School, unfortunately you will search the island's restaurants in vain for most of these dishes.

Some of the restaurants are at hotels where you might like to spend the night, especially if you want to have dinner there and there is no public transport back to base later in the evening.

THE RECIPES

Most of our recommended restaurants were willing to share with us the *ingredients* used in their recipes, but the actual preparation remains their 'secret' (in truth, they are simply not written down, but just passed on from cook to cook over the years). So you can rest assured that we have cooked *all* of the given recipes ourselves, to make sure they 'work'!

What we cannot guarantee, of course, is that they will taste as good back home as they did on Madeira! So many factors come into play to make food taste better when you are on holiday — from the intangibles (the atmosphere and the sense of relaxation after a day's good walking) to the tangible (hardness of the water, quality of the fish and other ingredients — even bananas!). So if you are in self-catering, why not try some of these recipes while you're on the island?

We've made all of these dishes on the simple kind of cooker usually found in self-catering (two rings and a decent oven) — or on a barbecue. And good news for anyone suffering food intolerances: all of the recipes can be **gluten- and dairy-free** (see page 136).

MADEIRAN FOOD

You will be hard-pressed to have a bad meal on the island if you seek out 'regional' (Madeiran) dishes. Top of our list would be **soup**: the ubiquitous tomato and onion, fresh vegetable (varied daily), or thick fish soups. **Fish** dishes are always reliable, from plain grills to *espada* with exotic

On virtually every café menu you will find *prego* (steak sandwich). The *prego* shown left is on *bolo do caco* (see page 82) — *not* a good idea, since the thick bread overwhelms the thin piece of steak; *prego* is far better on a simple roll *(papa seco)*. If you don't fancy a sandwich, there's always *prego no prato* (steak and fried egg on a plate, shown right) — with chips and salad.

fruit. **Beef** (including the speciality, *espetada*) ranges from perfection to shoe leather. There is no better beef than Madeiran, but *do* make sure your beef is sirloin *(lombo)* or fillet *(filete)*.

Pork and **chicken** also feature widely and are invariably best when grilled on open fires (as, for instance, at the Eira do Serrado or Curral das Freiras; see Walk 3). Do *not* expect to find many veal or lamb dishes, although some of our recommended restaurants do offer lamb cutlets.

We tend to give the **dessert** course a miss; in simple restaurants these are usually limited to *pudim* (a sort of crème caramel) or fruit. But some of our recommendations *do* have exotic sweets or cakes, mentioned on the mini-menus.

'**Madeira-style**' on a menu invariably means with tomato and onion … probably a bit of garlic, and perhaps oregano.

Table wines are imported from Portugal, with the exception of a few fairly new wines from vineyards in Porto Moniz and São Vicente, which

Portuguese wines

All supermarkets stock good wines from mainland Portugal. Some of our favourites are those from the mountains north of Oporto (including fortified ports):
• *Vinho Verde* ('green', or new wine): slightly sparkling quaffing wine — Aveleda, Casal Garcia, Gatão and Lagosta
• *Douro* — Esteva, Evel, Ferreirinho, Planalto, Porça de Murça
• *Bairrada* — Aliança, João Pires, José-Maria Fonseca BSE (Branco Seco Especial)
From further south, around Coimbra, there is a choice of:
Dão: reliable heavy reds — Grão Vasco, Terras Altas
Other perennial favourites come from areas closer to Lisbon:
• *Alentejo* — Monsaraz, Vinho do Monte, Porta da Ravessa
• *Ribatejo* — Serradayres
• *Setúbal* — Perequita
• *Beira* — Quinta do Cardo white
Glossary
consumo: ordinary wine; *reserva*: better quality; *garrafeira*: best quality; *tinto*: red; *branco*: white; *garrafa*: bottle; *batoque*: cork (in case you want to take it home!)

we have found both expensive and disappointing. See page 113 for a brief introduction to the fortified **madeira wines**.

And finally: most restaurant portions (especially in the inexpensive establishments) are *huge*. They won't mind you sharing a main course. And don't be surprised, in a country restaurant, to be served boiled potatoes, sweet potatos, rice and bread all with the same dish! Atkins-dieters beware!

PLANNING YOUR VISIT
When to go

The simple answer is — any time of year. The island does not experience such great fluctuations in temperature as the mainland. Winter days are often warm and sunny (up to 20°C), and even at the height of summer the air temperature does not usually rise above 25°C on the coast. But we would suggest avoiding June and early July, when the island is often covered by a low cloud 'hat' — the *capacete*.

An ideal time to travel is at low season (August till Christmas, January 2nd to Easter, and again after Easter until the end of May). Christmas and Easter are high-season — crowded and expensive. *Do* of course, reckon with some days of rain, especially in early spring and autumn.

Where to stay

There is a wide choice of accommodation of all grades all over the island. But for a short, week's break by public transport, it is best to stay around Funchal, from where the buses will take you to all the walks in this book.

Rather than an hotel, consider self-catering: just search 'apartments in Funchal' on the web; Google, for instance, throws up dozens of sites, including privately-owned second homes and hotels with self-catering facilities. There are also several sites dedicated to the island, like madeira-island.com, which have lists of apartments and villas to rent.

What to take

Pack simply! You don't have to 'dress', even for dinner, in any of the restaurants we recommend. Instead, concentrate on your walking gear.

While no special equipment is needed for any of the walks, proper **walking boots** are preferable to any other footwear. Many walks can be wet or slippery at some stage; good ankle support is essential, and you will also be glad of the water-proofing. Each person should carry a **small rucksack**, and *all year round* it is advisable to pack it with a **sunhat, first-aid kit, spare socks** and some **warm clothing**. A **long-sleeved shirt** and **long trousers** should be worn or carried, for sun protection and for making your way through encroaching vegetation (which may be wet and prickly). You should always carry a **mobile phone**; the **emergency** number on Madeira (as throughout the EU) is 112. Note: some walks require a **torch**!

Depending on the season, you may also need a **windproof, lightweight rainwear, fleece** and **gloves**. Optional items include **swimwear** and a Swiss Army knife (packed in your hold luggage, *not* hand-luggage, or it will be confiscated!). Mineral water is sold almost everywhere in plastic half-litre bottles; *it is imperative that each walker carries at least a half-litre of water — a full litre in hot weather.*

Planning your walks

Look over the walks in advance — if only to see if you will need a torch! The walks are specifically designed for access by the excellent local **bus** network ... so that you can enjoy a bottle of wine with lunch! But if you *do* want to hire a **car**, and the route is linear, you can usually

Broad beans drying beside a levada. They are eaten dry as a snack or rehydrated to make soups and stews.

leave your car at the end of the walk and take a bus to the start.

We have **graded our walks** for the deskbound person who nevertheless keeps reasonably fit. None of these walks ascends more than about 300m/1000ft, although there are a few steep descents. Remember that these are *neat walking times;* it would be wise to *double the time,* to allow for nature-watching and stopping for a meal.

Our walking **maps** are based on the latest 1:50,000 two-sheet map of the island published in 1995 by the Portuguese Instituto Geográfico e Cadastral (now woefully out of date) and our own research in the intervening years. We have enlarged our maps to a scale of 1:35,000 to include a bit more detail, but the only paths shown on our maps are those we *know* to be viable.

Walking safely depends in great part on *knowing what to expect and being properly equipped*. For this reason we urge you to read through the *whole* walk description at your leisure *before* setting out, so that you have a mental picture of each stage of the route and the landmarks. A few of the routes are **signposted** or **waymarked** with red and yellow flashes (two horizontal stripes mean *continue this way*; X means *do not go this way*). On *most* of these walks you will encounter other people — an advantage if you get into difficulty. Nevertheless, we advise you **never** to walk alone.

ON ARRIVAL
Tourist information
There is a small tourist information office at the airport (often unstaffed), where you can pick up leaflets. The main tourist office is on Avenida Arriaga (1 on the Funchal plan) and open Mon-Fri 09.00-20.00, Sat-Sun 09.00-18.00; ℂ 225 658. Do stop by to pick up some free island maps, list of events, and a **bus timetable** (available at nominal cost).

There are many pretty outdoor cafés in Funchal, where you can take a break from shopping.

City bus pass
Horarios do Funchal are the operators of the orange **town buses**, and you'll be amazed how far they will take you! If you're staying for a week, the best bargain is a **7-day pass** (15 €) offering unlimited journeys throughout all zones. *You must present your passport.*

Otherwise, keep change handy and pay the drivers as you board (1,3 € per journey for the inner zone).

The passes are available at several kiosks along the Avenida do Mar (see plan; manned from 08.30 to 18.00 daily). But the 'Horarios' also have an office (open 11.00-13.00 and 17.00-21.00 Mon-Fri and 11.00-13.00 Sat) in the Anadia Shopping Center (10 on the plan). You can download any of their **timetables** *in advance:* www.horariosdofunchal.pt.

Shopping for self-catering

Madeiran bananas fail EU beauty contests but are sweet and delectable.

Although more exotic shopping trips will come later, make your first port of call the nearest **supermarket**, to stock up on essentials. Our favourite supermarkets in central Funchal are shown on the plan (at 10 and 21), but there are others just outside the centre and in the larger villages. Aside from staples, you may want to pick up a few extra things that might be missing from your base — like a vegetable peeler, a whisk … or batteries.

All the supermarkets have separate sections for delicatessen items, butchers and fishmongers, as well as bakeries. So this is an easy option if you're shopping in the afternoon or on a Sunday, when local markets aren't usually open. (Most supermarkets on the

island are now open all day, even on
Sundays.)

'Regional' produce

The supermarket shopping list (right) is
just for staples, but in case you are buying
fresh produce as well, here are a few tips.

There are three main supermarket
chains: Pingo Doce, Modelo and Sã. In our
experience, all are brilliant for buying
anything from a packet of crisps to a TV or
toaster. But we have listed them in order of
quality of fresh produce: Pingo Doce is
definitely the best in this respect and Sã is
often downright poor.

Be careful in supermarkets (and even
countryside *mini-mercados*) to buy *fresh
Madeiran produce,* as a lot of EU produce is
also on sale and, at first glance, may look
more attractive. Potatoes are an example.
Madeiran potatoes are bagged together in
all sizes, unwashed, and can look a little
grubby. The skin is thick, and the potatoes
tend to feel soft when you peel them. *But
they are fantastic,* and cook beautifully —
boiled, roasted, puréed, chipped or baked.

Madeiran produce is usually identified
as 'regional'. If in doubt, point to the item

> Supermarket shopping
>   list reminder
> washing-up liquid or
>   dishwasher tablets
> paper towels
> aluminium foil
> soap
> tissues/toilet paper
> scouring pads
> salt & pepper
> mineral water
> milk/cream*
> coffee/tea/drinking
>   chocolate
> butter*
> sugar
> bread*
> juice
> wine/beer/cider
> olive oil & vinegar
> eggs
> tomato purée
> rice
> mayonnaise/mustard
> torch batteries?
> vegetable peeler?
> whisk?
>
> *see gluten- and
> dairy-free alterna-
> tives on page 138

and ask if it is 'ray-jee-oh-**nahl**'. If it isn't, you may pay considerably more, and you will certainly eat less well.

Mercado dos Lavradores, from top to bottom, left to right: tuna and slinky black *espada* (both a must; they will fillet the *espada* for you); colourful moray eel and dried cod *(bacalhau)* – dare you try either of these? Vegetables and (below) a fanciful display of exotic fruits

Mercado dos Lavradores

Once the staples are in the cupboard, the real shopping fun can begin. It is worth getting up early to visit Funchal's **market** (29 on the plan). It opens Mon-Sat at 07.00 and is a feast for the eyes. Spend a while looking round first, to see what's on offer, then go back to the stalls where you want to buy. The market closes at 16.00 Mon-Thur and 15.00 on Saturdays. If you want to shop quite late, go on a Friday, when it's open till 20.00.

This breathtaking 15-20 minute 'flight' is the
perfect start to a day sightseeing around Monte.
You can return to Funchal by the famous 2km-long
'toboggan run' or by bus — or you can use the
upper cable car station as the starting point for
Walks 1 or 2.

monte cable car

EXCURSION

The ride begins at the **lower cable car station** at the eastern end of the Avenida do Mar (37 on the plan). Tickets are fairly pricey, but the panoramic views are worth every euro. Perhaps the most dramatic part of the 'flight' comes as the car rises over the motorway, with views straight down into the green corridor of the João Gomes Valley (Walk 1).

The ride ends at the **upper cable car station** (with café) at **Babosas**, just east of Monte. As you alight, you may be handed a leaflet advertising a 'light lunch' at the five-star **Quinta do Monte** (see page 19). If you are not planning to come back here for lunch or tea, turn *right* outside the

Transport: 🚡 cable car from Funchal to Babosas (near Monte); daily 10.00-18.00 except in strong winds/storms); 15-20min each way ☏ 780 280; www.madeiracablecar.com Return the same way (buy a return ticket, it's less expensive) or by frequent town 🚌 20 or 21 from Monte or town 🚌 22 from Babosas — or by toboggan (see below)

Refreshments en route:
Quinta do Monte (see page 19)
Monte Palace Gardens (café)
Cafés at the cable car station and in Monte

Points of Interest:
Monte Church (Nossa Senhora do Monte)
Monte Palace Tropical Garden; Mon-Sat 09.00-18.00; closed holidays ☏ 782 339
Babosas Chapel (Nossa Senhora da Conceição) and balcony viewpoint
'Toboggan ride' *(Carros de cesto)*; daily 09.00-18.00 (13.00 Sundays). Not 1/1, Good Friday, 15-16/8, 25/12

cable car station, to enjoy the view Babosas Balcony. Otherwise, turn *left* outside the cable car station. Following the agapanthus-lined Caminho das Babosas, you'll pass the hotel entrance on the right. Even if you don't take up their lunch offer, *do* visit the gardens — entrance is free.

Public gardens at Monte (left), setting off on the toboggan run (right); below: decorating Monte Church for the Feast of the Assumption (15/16 August)

Just opposite, on the left, is the entrance to the **Monte Palace Tropical Garden**, created during the late 1980s by a Madeiran who made his fortune in South Africa. Again, the entry price is fairly steep, but you can spend hours here admiring the wealth of tropical and indigenous plants, not to mention the wonderful ceramic tiles and a host of minor follies.

Further along the lane is the starting point for the **toboggan run**, just below **Monte Church**, where Madeiran pilgrims pray to the tiny poignant statue of Our Lady of the Assumption, the island's patron saint. Beyond the church are the **public gardens**, a delight of topiary laid out below the ivy-covered viaduct of

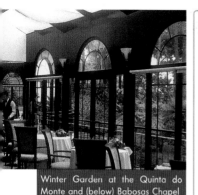

Winter Garden at the Quinta do Monte and (below) Babosas Chapel

QUINTA DO MONTE
Largo das Babosas (780 100
www.quintamonte.com
daily, all day €–€€

3-course '**light lunch**' — soup or salad, steak with potatoes and fresh vegetables, tropical fruit salad €€

superb **snack menu** from 2,50 € — including a dozen different sandwiches, toasted sandwiches, salads, cakes, hot snacks like crepes, omelettes, quiche and spaghetti

drinks from 2,50 €. The hot chocolate is a perfect warmer before setting off on Walks 1 or 2.

the old funicular railway that once ran between Monte and Funchal. In the **main square** plane trees shade a bandstand, cafés, souvenir stalls and taxis galore.

Head back east from the square, to return by toboggan, cable car or bus from Babosas — or to carry on with Walk 1 or 2. We highly recommend stopping for a snack, lunch or tea at the Quinta do Monte. Even if you're wearing walking boots, you will be welcome in the gardens or the tile-floored Winter Garden (pictured).

Babosas is just a plane-shaded square with a lovely 19th-century chapel, a bus shelter, and a superb viewpoint over **Curral dos Romeiros** (see photograph on page 20).

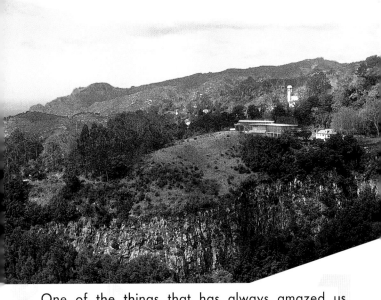

One of the things that has always amazed us about Madeira is how close you can be to dense housing yet come upon a primeval landscape just around a fold in the hillside. This walk is a perfect example; it explores the 'Green Corridor' created by the awesome João Gomes Valley.

ribeira de joão gomes

WALK

The walk starts from the **upper cable car station** at **Babosas**. When you leave the glassed-in station, turn right. (But if you first want to visit Monte or have a warming drink at the Quinta do Monte, turn left; see page 19.) Almost at once you come to a balcony viewpoint overlooking the wild, deep João Gomes Valley — where you are heading.

Walk down the cobbled path between the chapel shown on page 19 and the viewpoint (various signs, including 'Levada dos Tornos', 'Bom Sucesso'). Some 350m/ yds below Babosas, you come to a fork (**7min**). The main walk keeps left here on an earthen path signed 'Levada dos Tornos'. *(Those who don't have a head for heights might like to follow the main walk 90m/300ft up to the levada, to see the setting and the waterfall. Then return to this fork to continue. Otherwise, curl right downhill now, keeping to the main cobbled trail with street lights. Follow this across a bridge over the João Gomes River, then rise*

Distance: 6km/3.7mi; 2h35min

Grade: moderate, but with a steep descent of 400m/1300ft (mostly on steps). *Not suitable after rain.* Short initial ascent to the Levada dos Tornos (90m/300ft). You must be sure-footed and have a head for heights; possibility of vertigo on the Tornos levada (but this section can be omitted; see notes at the 7min-point).

Equipment: stout lace-up shoes or walking boots, warm clothing in cool weather, walking stick

Transport: 🚠 cable car (see page 17) or town 🚌 22 to Babosas. Return on town 🚌 7, 29, 30, 33, 34A, 36 or 47 from Bom Sucesso

Refreshments en route:
Quinta do Monte (see page 19) or café at the cable car station (both at the start of the walk)
bar at Bom Sucesso at the end

Points of Interest:
Babosas Chapel (Nossa Senhora da Conceição) and balcony viewpoint
Levada dos Tornos
'Green Corridor' flora

up the far side and fork right following the sign 'Levada do Bom Sucesso', to pick up the main walk again at the 1h05min-point.)

The main walk path climbs gently for 90m/300ft to join the **Levada dos Tornos** (see page 30) at the point where it emerges from a 1.5km/1mi-long tunnel — the shorter of two tunnels bringing water from a power station near Ribeiro Frio. Almost at once you walk under a spillway protecting the path from the lovely waterfall shown opposite. This part of the levada, where it rounds the head of the **Ribeira de João Gomes**, used to be horrendously vertiginous (see photo opposite).

People who strayed onto this part of the levada by mistake were often paralysed with fear. Now some railings provide psychological support, and there is plenty of vegetation at the side. Still, passing other walkers can be a fraught experience!

Eventually you leave this wilderness and come upon the first houses of **Romeiros** (**25min**). Keep on the levada until a building with a flagpole blocks the way. Take steps down to the right here, then go right on a cobbled trail with street lights (the same trail you were on when you left Babosas). A road joins you in a minute, then ends. A minute or two later you will see a sign for the Levada do Bom Sucesso on

Left: the Levada dos Tornos before the railings were built; right: waterfall carrying the João Gomes River into the lower valley.

your left. *Ignore it; keep to the trail.* Ten minutes later, turn left down another trail signposted to the Levada do Bom Sucesso (**1h05min**). *(Those who avoided the Tornos levada join here.)*

A log-stepped path now takes you quite steeply down the east side of the Ribeira de João Gomes, along the 'Green Corridor'. The dark forest of pine and eucalyptus is brightened by a myriad of mimosas and wild flowers in spring. Ten minutes down, a circular clearing is a pleasant place to pause. It's a good idea to take this opportunity to pack any loose bits away — there's a scramble coming up in a few minutes! Two minutes past the clearing, at a T-junction where your onward route is signposted to the left, go *right*. You'll quickly see the

lovely waterfall shown opposite, and it's not too difficult to scramble down to the pools in the river bed — a gorgeous place to paddle on a hot day.

Return to the T-junction and now go straight ahead. Soon you have fine views over to Babosas (photo page 20). Under 10 minutes down from the junction a path comes in from the left (the path you ignored just past Romeiros). A couple of yellow and red waymarks appear on this stretch, which is skiddy with rubble underfoot.

After crossing a **narrow bridge** (**1h55min**), you are finally following the elusive **Levada do Bom Sucesso**, today just an earthen balcony path with fantastic views to the expressway, the cable cars and the Bay of Funchal. It's likely that this path was created in part

The log-stepped descent to the Bom Sucesso levada. Left: waterfall and pool in the bed of the João Gomes River

for the schools; all around you textbook lessons in botany and geology come to life. *Watch your footing* as you pass below the **expressway** (**2h10min**); the path is very slippery, and it's tempting to just look ahead, to see how many buildings in town you can identify! All too soon you meet the end of a road (Rua Pita da Silva; **2h30min**): follow it to the left uphill, past the entrance to the **orchid garden** on the left. Then curl right downhill. The **bus shelter** (**2h35min**) is to your left; a **bar** to the right.

Londres

We can't even remember when or how we discovered our base restaurant in Funchal; you could walk past and not even notice it. But what we *did* notice, once inside, was that most of the clients were local. Now that it appears in several guides, tourists fill half the seats. Arrive early (before 7.30pm), book ahead, or wait for a table.

You can expect value for money, fresh food, fairly unremarkable meat dishes, and *simply superb fresh grilled fish.* The atmosphere is homely, the staff always friendly and helpful, never fussed by the bustle. On arrival you'll be greeted with a plate of marinated broad beans — just perfect with a dry white wine, *vinho verde,* beer or *sercial* aperitif. Whichever meal we choose, we often change our minds at the last minute and have the grilled *cherne,* our favourite. A word of warning: one serving is enough for two — especially if you have a first course — and they don't mind if you share.

Early evening at Londres; later on it will be throbbing!

LONDRES
Rua da Carreira 64A (**235 329**
Mon-Sat lunch and dinner €€

daily **main-course specials**; this menu is only printed in Portuguese, so ask them to translate for you; the grilled fresh fish dishes are *highly recommended.*

ten different **entrées**, from the obligatory tomato and onion soup to the exotically translated 'cockle duck style' (see page 28)!

wide range of **omelettes**

meats (usually grilled or fried), including beef (also *espetada*), liver, pork, lamb, chicken, turkey

simple **sweets** and ice creams

restaurants

eat

Over the years we've visited many of the restaurants in the capital, including those in the western 'tourist zone'. And you will be very unlucky if you have a bad meal.

One of the most pleasant places to make for is the Old Town, with many excellent restaurants, some with outside tables. Our only complaint there is that some of the busier ones are happy to lure you in, but then even happier to see you go so they can take another seating.

Grilled *cherne* at Londres — each tray holds a serving for one! Below: the Marina Terrace restaurant

We don't like to be rushed (you will *never* be rushed at Londres, no matter how busy).

Another idyllic setting (and it will be more so in future, when the commercial port moves east to the Porto Novo Valley) is the marina, with a string of very pleasant settings by the water's edge. If you start at the pier opposite Avenida Zarco and walk west, ignoring the blandishments of all the touts, we'll be surprised if you make it past Fernandes, who will lure you into the **Marina Terrace**. You won't regret it! The food is superb. Try their special steak — a very thick fillet served sizzling on a hot stone; they will slice it for you. The menu is huge, with fish and shellfish of all kinds and dishes to appeal to the kids as well — like pastas and excellent crunchy-crusted pizzas.

MEMORIES OF LONDRES

Broad bean appetizer *(favas)*

You want young (or frozen) broad beans for this dish, or the skins will be too tough. Cook as normal (15-20 minutes), then leave overnight covered in olive oil with some finely chopped onions and parsley (the Londres recipe does *not* call for garlic).

Another popular recipe is for *pickled* broad beans. Make a vinaigrette to the sharpness you like. Add 1 bay leaf, garlic, pepper, allspice and cloves to taste. Store the beans in a large screw-top jar.

'Cockles duck style' *(amêijoas à bulhão pato)*

Served at Londres, this is a very festive-looking dish! Allow about 15 cockles per person, and buy them on the day you will use them. Wash and scrub them clearn, then rinse them in 2-3 changes of cold water to remove the grit.

Prepare the rind of one lemon in julienne strips. Steam the cockles for 10 minutes or just until the shells open. (Some may take a minute or two longer, but remove any open cockles from the pan immediately.) *Discard any that do not open.* Pour over melted butter, some garlic juice and lemon juice. Sprinkle the lemon rind and parsley on top.

recipes

eat

There's no point in reproducing Londres' recipe for *cherne*, our favourite meal; it is simply very fresh wreckfish (stone bass), grilled with a bit of crushed garlic. Instead, here's a recipe for *the* most popular fish dish on the island, *espada com banana*, but with our twist — the bananas are caramelized. If you make too much, remember that cold left-over *espada* makes delicious sandwiches!

Espada with caramelized bananas (*espada com banana*)

First prepare any vegetables you are having with the meal, since the fish and bananas cook very quickly. Season the fillets with the salt, pepper, garlic and lemon juice. Dust with flour, dip in egg, then coat with breadcrumbs or ground almonds. Slice the bananas in half lengthwise.

Coat a suitably sized frying pan with 5mm/1/4" olive oil and heat to smoking, then lower the heat just a bit. (To make sure the temperature is right, toss in a tiny piece of bread; it should sizzle.) In a separate pan, gently heat the sugar and butter until just bubbling, stirring all the while, and making sure it doesn't burn!

Gently place the fillets in the oil and fry for just over two minutes each side, until golden brown. When turning the fish, place the bananas in the caramelized butter; the bananas will only take about two minutes to cook, and both should be just right at the same time. Serve at once!

Ingredients (for 4 people)
360 g *espada* fillets
6 small or Madeiran bananas
1 egg, beaten
salt, freshly ground pepper
1 clove of garlic, crushed
juice of one lemon
2 tbsp sugar
2 tbsp butter
breadcrumbs or ground almonds
flour for dusting
olive oil

Inaugurated in 1966, the Levada dos Tornos is Madeira's most important levada, with 106km (66mi) of main channels. This walk explores the levada in the primeval João Gomes Valley and then follows an easy stretch — past two tea houses — to Palheiro Ferreiro, where you can visit the splendid gardens (with café).

levada dos tornos

WALK

To **start the walk**, follow the notes for Walk 1 on page 21 and read the description of the levada path in the upper João Gomes Valley (with photograph on page 23). Then take care to make your decision at the fork reached in **7min**. Will you try the exciting but possibly vertiginous route, or opt for the main trail? (If you choose the main trail, just follow it down to the river and back up to the first village en route, where you will join a road. Watch for a building with a flagpole, on your left; then see the next paragraph.)

Whichever route you choose, the first habitation you reach is the village of **Romeiros** (**25min**), where a **building with a flagpole** (minus flag) sits astride the

Distance: 7.5km/4.6mi; 2h10min

Grade: easy, with an initial ascent of only 90m/300ft. The first part of the walk, in the upper João Gomes Valley, demands a head for heights, but this section can be omitted; see notes at the 7min-point.

Equipment: stout lace-up shoes or walking boots, warm clothing in cool weather, sunhat

Transport: cable car (see page 17) or town 22 to Babosas. Return from Palheiro Ferreiro on town 36 or 37. (Or end the walk at one of the two tea houses and return on town 47.)

Refreshments en route:
Quinta do Monte (at the start)
Hortensia Tea House (1h30min)
Jasmin Tea House (1h45min)
Palheiro Ferreiro (at the end)

Points of interest:
Babosas Chapel (Nossa Senhora da Conceição) and balcony viewpoint
Levada dos Tornos
Palheiro Gardens; Mon-Fri 09.30-16.30; closed holidays (793 044

levada. *If you came on the levada,* descend steps to the right here, then take the next set of steps back up to the left to regain the levada. *If you came by the trail,* turn left up the first set of concrete steps just past this building; at the top of the steps turn right.

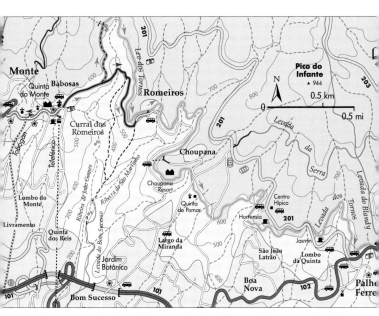

You are on the levada but, as in all villages, it is covered with concrete slabs. Soon you'll see the watercourse in full flow.

Now follow the meandering levada through groves of pine and mimosa, eventually passing through the grounds of the **Choupana Resort Hotel (50min)**, where you are asked to keep to the path. On meeting a crossing road (which leads south to the Jardim Botânico; **1h05min**), walk a few metres downhill to the right, then go through the doorway opposite (sign: Levada dos Tornos). A chapel is on your right; it belongs to the **Quinta do Pomar**, which you quickly pass.

In about **1h30min** you pass steps up left to a stop for town bus 47. Some 200m/yds further on, more steps lead up left to the **Hortensia Tea House**, in beautifully landscaped gardens. Stop to admire the plantings and perhaps limit your intake to an 'entrée' in the rustic house (their home-made vegetable soups are lovely); the next tea house is only 15 minutes away!

You cross the ER201 (**1h40min**) and, three minutes later, pass above the **Jasmin Tea House** — yet another chance for refreshment — beer and a toasted sandwich? Town bus 47 also departs from the bottom of their drive.

In **2h** you reach the ER102. Approach *carefully* — traffic roars round the blind bend to the left. Turn right on the road. The entrance to the **Palheiro Gardens** (**2h10min**) is several

Water for the Levada dos Tornos is collected from three chief sources in the north. It runs in open channels to a power station near Ribeiro Frio and from there flows through a very long tunnel (there are 16km/10mi of tunnels on the Tornos!) to the south of the island, emerging into the open again high in the João Gomes Valley — where we meet it on Walks 1 and 2. From there it meanders on to irrigate more than 100,000 outlets between Funchal and Santa Cruz.

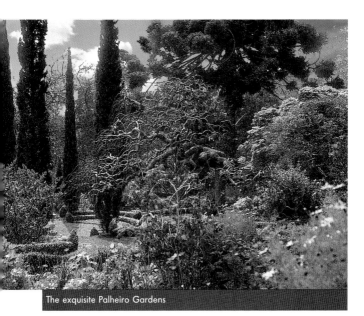
The exquisite Palheiro Gardens

minutes further downhill, on the left, almost opposite the ER201 to Terreiro da Luta (and another bus stop). The cobbled drive is shaded by plane trees and lined with lilies and camellias. Below the house (privately owned and closed to the public) gentle terraces yield up ever-changing vistas of the formal and informal landscaping, avenues and gardens surrounding the Count of Carvalhal's original *quinta* (now a five-star hotel) and chapel. Your final chance for refreshment is the snack bar/restaurant here (shared with the golfers), before you make your way to the nearest **bus stop**.

HORTENSIA GARDENS
daily except 25/12 from 10.00-18.00

special 'tea for two' €

salads, **vegetable soups**, **drinks** including non-alcoholic beer, *poncha* (local punch made from lemons, sugarcane spirit and sugar); sandwiches on **home-made bread**, **waffles** with home-made jam, **apple tart** with cream, **scones** (allow 15 minutes)

You're really spoilt for choice on this walk, wth two tea houses offering home cooking in idyllic settings. Both are intimate, homely places, with tables indoors and out. You'll meet other walkers, and perhaps plan some joint excursions! The Jasmin is currently up for sale, but we expect this long-established business to carry on as before.

JASMIN TEA HOUSE
daily except 25/12 from 10.00-18.00

salads, **vegetable soups**, wide range of **drinks**, including non-alcoholic beer; toasted **sandwiches**, country bread, **scones**, home-made **honey cake**

separate tea menu: **91 different teas**, including organic and herbal

Top: entrance to the Hortensia Tea House; below: Jasmin front garden, with views to Funchal

restaurants

eat

'REID'S' CAKE

'The' place to have tea on Madeira is, of course, Reid's Hotel. We used stay there on holiday. One day the hall porter suggested that we go out for a walk — and that was the spark that ignited Sunflower Books many years later.

We returned to Madeira once or twice a year for almost a decade, until we had enough material to publish the first edition of *Landscapes of Madeira.* We loved the fruit cake served at tea but, once bitten by the hiking bug, we were never there for tea any more! So on each visit the hall porter always greeted us on arrival with a *whole* rich fruit cake. We called it 'Reid's' Cake'.

Wrapped in brown paper, this could be kept in our room without spoiling for up to three weeks! We had 'tea' on the levadas, always with a slice of that magnificent cake, the perfect hikers' fuel.

The days when we could afford to spend a month at Reid's are long past, but we do have a brilliant rich fruit cake recipe (see credit on page 140) and always make it at home, then take it to Madeira.

Nowadays there are lovely places all around the island to have tea. Apart from the Hortensia and the Jasmin, one of the best is O Fio at Ponta do Pargo (see pages 121-123), where the herbs for their tisane are grown in pots on the front terrace.

recipes

eat

'Reid's' Cake

Preheat the oven to 180°C, 350°F, gas mark 4.

Grease a 900 g (2 lb) bread loaf tin and line it with non-stick foil (including the corners). Make sure the foil is smooth.

In a large bowl, mix together the flour, sugar, dried fruit, cherries, nuts and mixed spice.

Add the remaining, liquid ingredients and beat the mixture until everything is thoroughly mixed.

Using a flexible spatula, place the mixture in the prepared tin, smooth the surface with a wet knife, and bake in the preheated oven for two hours — or until a skewer inserted into the middle of the cake comes out clean.

Allow to cool completely before removing from the tin. The cake will keep for weeks if wrapped in foil or brown paper and stored in a cool, dry place.

Ingredients (for about 12 servings)

300 g self-raising flour*
300 g granulated sugar*
700 g mixed dried fruit
75 g glacé cherries, chopped
50 g mixed nuts, chopped
1 tsp mixed spice
3 medium eggs, beaten
2 tbsp vegetable oil
250 ml water
1 tbsp black treacle or molasses

*see page 140 for notes about g-f, d-f substitutions

Until the 1950s the post (with vital funds sent home by emigrants) was carried from Funchal to Curral by a woman. Climbing and descending via the Eira do Serrado, with her precious deliveries balanced in a basket on her head, she counted 52 hairpin bends each way. This walk follows the easiest part of her daily round.

curral das freiras

WALK

Start out at the **Eira do Serrado** car park. First climb the aloe-fringed path at the left of the beautifully-situated hotel; it leads to the famous viewpoint. Then return and descend the steps at the right of the sign 'Eira do Serrado Alt. 1094 m' (**15min**).

The steps lead into a beautiful old cobbled trail below chestnut trees. Sweet chestnut *(Castanea sativa)* groves have been cultivated on the island since the earliest days of settlement. Not only did the fruit provide food for the population, but the wood had many uses (you'll see a lot of vines in this area on chestnut-wood trellises).

You clear the trees five minutes down, to be greeted by more superb views — and down here you won't have to share them! As the trail makes a V-turn to the left, you are just level with the entrance to

Distance: 3.3km/2mi; 1h30min

Grade: moderate descent of 450m/ 1475ft. In autumn and winter fallen chestnut leaves obscure the path, so watch your footing. Short ascent.

Equipment: stout lace-up shoes or walking boots, warm clothing in cool weather, sunhat

Transport: 🚌 81 to the Eira turn-off on the ER107 (add 10min walking), or by 🚐 to the Eira do Serrado viewpoint. Return on 🚌 81 — back to Funchal, or to the Eira turn-off, to collect your car (add 10min walking)

Alternative walk: Levada do Curral. At the end of the walk, *sure-footed* walkers could explore the top end of the Levada do Curral, one of the most beautiful on the island. The path is only 30cm/12" wide at best (see photograph overleaf), with sheer drops almost immediately and *no* protective railings. Those *with a very good head for heights* could follow it south for about an hour.

Refreshments en route:
Estalagem Eira do Serrado (at the start)
Vale das Freiras (at the end)

Points of interest:
Eira do Serrado viewpoint
Curral das Freiras
chestnuts!

Pico Grande from the Eira do Serrado viewpoint

the old road tunnel under the Eira. In contrast to the tunnels built today with massive boring machines financed by the EU, this tunnel (opened in 1959) was man-made — hacked out of the rock with picks. (It is ironic to note that road construction workers are still regularly killed on the island today, despite the plethora of EU health and safety regulations.)

On the far side of the Ribeira do Curral, the houses of Casas Próximas teeter on the *lombo* plunging off Pico do Serradinho. As you descend close by the old road, you'll be a source of some amusement to passing motorists. S-bends take you past a couple of well-placed promontories, one of them with an electricity pylon (**45min**). From here there is a view back left to Pico Grande, John's favourite mountain. Contrast this view with the one seen from the Folhadal walk (Walk 10). Pico Grande is easily recognisable from many parts of the island because of the prominent protrusion at the summit.

Beyond this promontory the path, narrow in places, continues to drop sharply in more S-bends. In summer the surrounding cliffs are bright with yellow-flowering houseleeks. Soon you're just opposite Curral's church. When the road is not

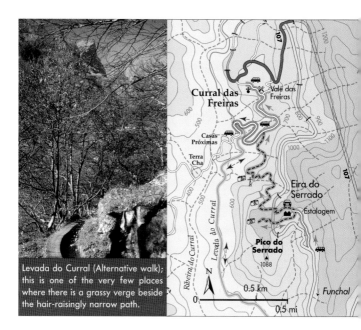

Levada do Curral (Alternative walk); this is one of the very few places where there is a grassy verge beside the hair-raisingly narrow path.

far below you, notice that the path *climbs;* don't try to scramble down too soon. Once on the road (**1h15min**), you could turn left downhill to the nearest bus stop (5min) or descend for just under 15 minutes to the Levada do Curral, on the left, opposite another bus stop (Alternative walk).

But we'd suggest you walk 800m uphill (15min) to the Vale das Freiras restaurant in **Curral das Freiras** (**1h30min**), for some unforgettable chestnut soup and cake, and take a bus from outside the church.

Whether or not you like chestnuts, this walk has two splendid opportunities for a light snack or a very substantial meal. Evening buses back from Curral would even allow you to have an early dinner. (Better still, spend a night at the Estalagem Eira do Serrado and treat yourself!) If you *do* like chestnuts, Curral is nirvana!

Vale das Freiras

This long-established restaurant, a favourite with walkers, has recently doubled in size, with a huge open fire where you can watch your chicken or steak being grilled. Or you may prefer to eat on one

VALE DAS FREIRAS
Curral das Freiras (712 177
daily, all day €

wide variety of **salads** (including octopus) and **omelettes**

pasta spirals and spaghetti

meats: beef (including *espetada*), pork chops, chicken — grilled on an open fire

fish (cod, sardines, *espada*, octopus), mixed **shellfish** *paella*

chestnut specialities: soup, salad, omelette, cake, liqueurs

of the terraces, with views up to the Eira and surrounding mountains. The portions are hearty, and the food is delicious. Every guest is offered a free home-made liqueur to sample; they have a very large selection — including, of course, chestnut!

restaurants

eat

Estalagem Eira do Serrado

If you love mountains then, without doubt, this hotel has the best views on the island. Breakfast on the terrace of your superbly-appointed room, before the crowds arrive, is unforgettable. But

ESTALAGEM EIRA DO SERRADO
Eira do Serrado ℂ **710 060**
www.eiradoserrado.com
daily, all day €–€€

huge menu, with 20 different **entrées**, steaks, chicken, pork, fish and shellfish — all grilled or sauced.

regional specialities *available most Sundays or on special order (telephone two days in advance):* lamb, roast suckling pig, rabbit casserole, roast goat, stuffed turkey, and *cozido* (pork and vegetable stew)

wide variety of **sweets**; chestnut specialities and liqueurs

bar with snacks, chestnut cake, etc

if you've no time to spend a night here, then *do* come for a meal. The dining room sits at the edge of the cliff, with magnificent plummeting views into Curral. Remember that if you come for Sunday lunch, you should be able to choose one of the regional specialities without having to order two days in advance. *A must!*

OVERDOSE ON CHESTNUTS!

Chestnut soup *(sopa de castanha)*

Unless you are using prepared chestnuts, first see notes in the first paragraph of the recipe opposite. In a heavy-bottomed saucepan, heat the oil, toss in the bacon bits and onion, and fry gently until golden.

Add all the other ingredients and bring to the boil. Reduce the heat and simmer for about an hour, or until the vegetables are soft. Serve topped with the parsley.

Hint: If you have a barbecue where you are based, you may like to visit the chestnut factory in Curral (past the church, at the top end of the village) and buy some fresh chestnuts to roast at home.

Roasted chestnuts and chestnut soup at the Vale das Freiras

Ingredients (for 4 people)
1.5 l vegetable stock or bouillon
1 cup of fresh or packaged chestnuts
0.5 kg potatoes, cut in pieces
2 medium sweet potatoes, cut in pieces
2 medium carrots, quite thickly sliced
1 medium onion, chopped
4 tbsp bacon bits ('lardons')
2 tbsp olive oil
fresh flat parsley
salt and pepper to taste

recipes

eat

Chestnut cake
(bolo de castanha)

If you are using dried chestnuts, soak them overnight and cook until tender (about an hour). If using fresh, boil them for a few minutes, skin them, then boil for about another 20 minutes.

Preheat the oven to 160°C, 325°F, gas mark 3. Prepare a loose-bottomed 20 cm/8 " circular cake tin by greasing thoroughly.

Cream the chestnuts in a blender (if you don't have one, mash them very finely with whatever is to hand!). In a separate container, beat the egg yolks and sugar; add the baking powder and vanilla. Add this mixture to the chestnut purée.

Beat the egg whites until they form soft peaks, then gently fold into the cake mixture.

Cook the cake in the preheated oven for 35min, or until a skewer inserted into the middle comes out clean.

Ingredients (for 10 servings)
300 g fresh or prepared chestnuts
125 g granulated sugar
4 eggs, separated
1 tsp baking powder
1 tsp vanilla

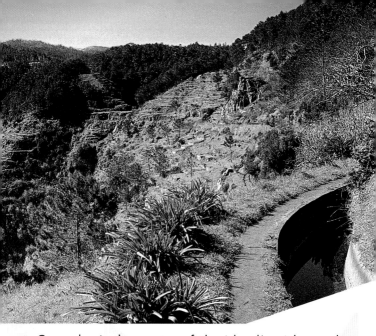

Camacha is the centre of the island's wickerwork industry; Santo da Serra is known for its many fine *quintas*. The Levada da Serra (easy strolling) lies above both villages, and the Levada dos Tornos (fairly vertiginous) below. Why not set two days aside to enjoy both routes?

camacha and santo da serra

WALK

Walk 1 introduced the Levada dos Tornos in no uncertain terms! You can follow another stretch of this gorgeous water-course beginning at Camacha and ending at Santo da Serra. But this time there are no railings, and some sections are vertiginous. We hope you *can* manage it, because it is a beautiful walk, and far less visited than the section followed in Walk 2.

But another levada runs not far above these two hill villages. It doesn't carry water any longer (its flow has all been diverted to the Tornos 200m/650ft below). Today it is just a wide trail shaded by mature forest and brightened in summer by a blaze of hydrangeas and agapanthus. This is the Levada da Serra, one of the first to be built on the island.

The ideal way to do this walk would be to take the

On the Tornos (see page 48)

Distance: 16km/10mi; 4h45min

Grade: Easy, but fairly long. You *must be sure-footed and have a head for heights.* You may have to walk *through* ice-cold (seasonal) waterfalls. Short ascent at the end.

Equipment: stout shoes (walking boots preferable), sunhat, plenty of water, snacks, warm clothing all year round, long trousers, whistle, **torch**

Transport: 🚌 29 or 77 to Camacha; 🚌 77 from Santo da Serra

Refreshments: restaurants and cafés in Camacha and Santo da Serra; *nothing en route*

Points of interest:
wickerwork at Camacha
quintas at Santo da Serra
the levada and its surroundings

On the Serra (see page 51)

Distance: 17.5km/11mi; 5h

Grade: easy, after an initial climb of 150m/490ft, although quite long

Equipment: as above, but stout shoes will suffice; no torch needed

Transport, refreshments, points of interest: as above (but to avoid 1h of road-walking, start at Águas Mansas; see footnote page 51)

47

Palm tree shortly after joining the Levada dos Tornos

Tornos from Camacha to Santo da Serra and, another day, the Serra back to Camacha (where you could stock up on wickerwork!).

Both routes start in **Camacha**'s main square (the Achada da Camacha). First take a peep at the magnificent wickerwork in the Café/ Estalagem do Relógio. When you leave the shop, the Tornos route lies in the south and the Serra route (description overleaf) to the north.

For the Tornos route: *Facing* the Café do Relógio, descend the road on the right (signposted to Funchal); you pass the new village church on your left. Ignore a small road off right, cross the Camacha bypass and continue down the steep road almost opposite (just to the right). In **7min** fork right, then look left for a fine view over the Porto Novo Valley. A few minutes later, at a T-junction, turn left. Now watch for where this road crosses the **Levada dos Tornos** (by a small parking bay; **14min**) and turn left on the levada.

Before long (**23min**) you pass a house with the magnificent **palm tree** shown above; a road runs along on the right here. Keep up on the levada, and you will come to a **tunnel** a minute

Notes for this route continue on page 53

N

0.5 km

0.5 mi

Sítio das 4 Estradas

Portela

João Frino

102

Curral Velho

Santo da Serra

52

Levada do Pico

Levada da Serra

Levada dos Tornos

700

1000

900

Ribeiro Serrão

Cancela

Casa florestal

Águas Mansas

Boqueirão

52

da do Pico do Arvoredo

800

Eira de Fora

102

Eiroses

ras do Rochão

Levada dos

Tornos

500

Eiroses 763

Pico de Gaula

Lombo Grande

206

Caminho Municipal da Portela

Rochão

600

Achadinha

700

O Cesto

taxi

Camacha

Ribeira do Porto Novo

400

Casais de Além

Relógio

Levada da Serra

800

700

500

300

Vale do Paraíso

Camacha Shopping

102

Ribeirinha

03

Ribeira do Caniço

205

Laboratório Agrícola Caniço

For the Serra route*:
With your back to the
Café do Relógio, cross
the square and walk
north uphill on the road
signposted to Santo da
Serra. You pass the res-
taurants 'O Cesto' on
the left and 'O Boléu'
on the right (see page
56). Then climb the

Hydrangeas (above) and oaks (left) flank the dry Levada da Serra

narrow road just north of Camacha's old church (the Caminho
Municipal da Portela, with walkers' signposts on the left).

When you reach the crossing **Levada da Serra** (under
15min), turn right and just stride out (or stroll along),
eventually crossing the road to Poiso and Pico do Arieiro
(ER202; about **3h**). Some 1h15min later you cross a track and
come to the **Santo da Serra waterhouse** (**4h15min**). Enjoy its
shady pines and charming gardens, then return to the track and
descend to the ER102 (25min). Turn right downhill, then turn
left into **Santo da Serra** (20min; **5h**). Restaurante A Nossa
Aldeia (see page 57) is not far past the petrol station, on a side
road to the left — an unmissable, bright pink building.

*This levada has been covered by a road in the Porto Novo Valley (3km). To
avoid asphalt and save about 1h30min, take 🚌 77 to Águas Mansas. From the
junction of the ER206 and the ER102, walk 100m/yds north towards Santo da
Serra, then turn left up a road. Past a forestry house, the road reverts to track.
Keep left at a fork, then fork right uphill on a path beside the rushing Levada do
Pico. When you reach the (dry) Levada da Serra in 10 minutes, turn right.

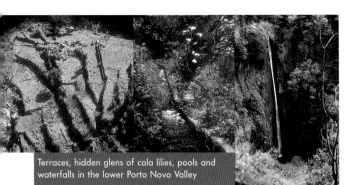

Terraces, hidden glens of cala lilies, pools and waterfalls in the lower Porto Novo Valley

Tornos route (continued from page 48)

later, where you will need your torch for three minutes. Another **tunnel** is met in **40min** (two minutes; no torch needed). Beyond this tunnel there is a possibility of vertigo: although the path is very adequate, there is *no* protective fencing, and the drops are severe — perhaps 50m/150ft. Often ice-cold waterfalls cascade onto the path as well, and you may get soaked. Watch out, too, for the concrete blocks in the path, supporting the pipe carrying some of the water. But this part of the walk, in the lower part of the **Ribeira do Porto Novo**, is one of the most beautiful stretches of the Tornos. Suddenly birds and cascades are singing everywhere. In **50min** the levada makes a U-turn high in the valley, below some pools. The waterfall shown above crashes into the river; all else is stillness. This is an idyllic rest spot.

Go through the third and shortest **tunnel** (**1h**), then skirt round a **tunnel with 'windows'** (**1h10min**). *Be sure to climb up steps beyond this tunnel to rejoin the Tornos;* the levada ahead runs

Boaventura Valley in early autumn

down to Gaula. Soon you reach a reservoir at **Lombo Grande** (**1h30min**) and then the ER206. If you need an 'escape route', turn right and descend for a minute to a bus stop, where bus 60 leaves for Funchal at noon (not Sundays).

Crossing straight over the road, in under ten minutes you have good views over the airport and São Lourenço Point. After 20 minutes you pass through a very short **tunnel** (no torch is needed, but it is very low: watch your head!) and come out in the **Ribeira da Boaventura**. While the Porto Novo is our favourite part of the Tornos in spring, in summer the Boaventura Valley takes the prize. The terraces are golden with wheat, and the levada paths are aglow with blue and white agapanthus — so tall and thick that they are almost like hedgerows. You progress quite easily for a good 20 minutes past the tunnel, but then the way becomes vertiginous, as it delves into a very deep tributary, the **Ribeira dos Vinháticos**. By **2h20min** you reach the head of this stream. The next, smaller tributary, is a basin full of willow.

In just over **3h05min** you pass a waterhouse on the left; beyond it is a road. Two minutes later a second road is crossed (**3h10min**). Both lead up to the ER102 at João Frino, if you're pressed for time and trying to catch bus 77. Beyond the second road you delve into the upper reaches of a new valley — the

Ribeira de Santa Cruz. Ignore all the cobbled trails and paths crossing the levada during the next 45 minutes or so; civilisation seems very far away, as you enter an emerald wilderness.

Then suddenly, at **3h55min**, the levada ends. Unbelievable! How can this magnificent watercourse, which has carried you through the most beautiful valleys in the southeast, have abandoned you without warning? Its waters shoot out into a tank some 200m/650ft below, to feed the Levada Nova. A **pipe** coming in from the Levada da Serra runs down and over to the *lagoa* (reservoir) above Santo da Serra.

Walk back along the levada for six minutes, then turn right up cobbled steps. A few minutes uphill, you emerge in fields. Head towards the electricity wires in front of you, keeping to the left of the plots. At a stone wall, bear left. Bear left again at a second wall, quickly coming to a cobbled track. Go left uphill (past the entrance to a *quinta*), to a crossroads.

Turn right here, for the final stretch into Santo da Serra. You first skirt the grounds of this mysterious *quinta*, overgrown with luxuriant vegetation. For a short time in the 1800s it was home to a young Scottish doctor, Robert Reid Kalley, esteemed by the islanders for his near-miraculous cures. But he was also a Protestant, and when the authorities would no longer tolerate his incessant proselytising, he had to flee dressed as a woman.

At a fork, be sure to keep right. Cross the **Ribeira Serra de Água** and rise through housing, where tar comes underfoot. This road takes you into **Santo da Serra** (**4h45min**). Turn left to Restaurante A Nossa Aldeia (see page 57) — a pink building on a road to the right, not far past the **church**.

O Cesto

You can get a drink or snack in the bar here from 10am to 10pm, but the restaurant is only open for lunch (from 12.00 to 16.00). The meals, served in a very comfortable, large dining room, are delicious (see next pages for two of their specialities), and the wine list more than adequate.

Almost opposite is **O Boléu**, also serving home-cooked fare (especially delicious soups). Both restaurants serve the excellent local bread.

O CESTO
Camacha (just south of the old church) (922 068
bar daily 10.00-22.00 €
restaurant daily except Thur 12.00-16.00 €
bar for light snacks, including sandwiches of tongue, *espada*, steak

restaurant serving substantial home-cooked fare with Madeiran/Portuguese specialities including *carne de vinho e alhos* and *frango na púcara* (see page 59).

Fanciful wickerwork on display at the Café/Estalagem do Relógio

You need never go hungry in Camacha! The **Relógio** in the main square is also an hotel and always open. Its menu (regional and international) is simply huge. It's a bit pricier than the Cesto or Boléu.

restaurants

eat

A Nossa Aldeia

Although there are hotels in Santo da Serra, the locals inevitably congregate around the long, shared tables at this very simple, homely restaurant — usually to tuck into *espetada* and *milho frito*.

A NOSSA ALDEIA
Santo da Serra (552 142
daily except Mon lunch and dinner €

soups, **egg dishes** and **omelettes** are the only light dishes; no salads or sandwiches

fish is limited to *espada* with tartar sauce and *bacalhau* (dried cod)

meats include the usual grilled beef, pork and chicken dishes; but also **tongue in wine sauce** and **picadinho** (sauteed pork or beef — you choose — with chips)

very adequate **wine list** for a restaurant in this category

You can hardly miss A Nossa Aldeia — a bright pink building. The fire where they cook the *espetada* is behind the waitress in the top photo.

It's not the most comfortable of restaurants, as seating is on wooden benches. But the rustic decor and friendly service, large portions and low prices compensate — especially after a long walk!

For more sophisticated surroundings, try one of the hotels (but, unfortunately, we found the hotel A Quinta disappointing). If you want to walk a bit further (or have a car), we've been told that Dias Felices, 300 m south of the village on the ER102, is *the* new 'in' place!

HEARTY HILL-VILLAGE FARE

Meat (pork) with wine and garlic *(carne de vinho e alhos)*

This dish must be prepared a few days in advance. Roll the pork cubes in the salt and refrigerate overnight. Transfer the meat to an

oven-proof casserole, pour over the marinade, cover, and refrigerate for three to four days.

Preheat the oven to 150°C, 300°F, gas mark 2. On top of the stove, bring the meat and marinade just to the boil, then transfer to the oven. Cover and cook for 1h, then allow to cool.

Skim off the fat and heat in a large frying pan. Fry the meat over a quite high flame, turning, until all sides are golden *(Do not crowd the pan, or the meat will steam. Keep cooked cubes warm in the oven.)* If there is not enough fat, add some lard. If the sauce reduces too much, slowly add more wine.

This dish is traditionally served with boiled *and* sweet potatoes and orange slices. It may also be served with fried bread that has been pre-soaked in the marinade (you would need to *double* the marinade ingredients).

Ingredients (for 4 people)
700 g loin of pork with
   plenty of fat, cut into
   3 cm cubes
coarse salt
lard

For the marinade:
250 ml white wine
100 ml vinegar
black pepper
6 cloves garlic, crushed
1 bay leaf

recipes

eat

Chicken in a pot *(frango na púcara)*

Easy to prepare, this O Cesto speciality originated in mainland Portugal. Our recipe is just one of *many* variations; some add *aguardente,* shallots or white wine; others omit the red pepper.

Preheat the oven to 180°C, 350°F, gas mark 4. Fry the chicken pieces in 2 mm of olive oil until golden on all sides. Pat dry on paper towels. Remove to a heavy casserole, add the other ingredients (pre-mixed), and cook, covered, for 40 minutes. Uncover and cook for another 20 minutes, by which time the sauce will have reduced nicely.

Serve with rice or boiled potatoes and vegetables, or with sweet potato bread (see page 92) and a simple salad.

Ingredients (for 4 people)
1 chicken (1.5 kg), jointed
olive oil (for frying the chicken)
150 ml vegetable stock
100 ml port or madeira wine
1 tin (400 g) chopped tomatos
1 tsp Dijon mustard
100 g Portuguese sausage *(chouriço),* sliced
2 tbsp diced sweet red pepper
2 cloves garlic, crushed

This is a five-star walk to which we return again and again, to enjoy the wonderful play of light and shade along the Levada do Furado, the limpid pools of the Levada do Bezerro, and the centuries-old trails around Ribeiro Frio — to say nothing of a trout lunch!

around ribeiro frio

WALK

Begin the walk just below the **Restaurante Ribeiro Frio**, where you will see a signpost to Portela on your right (further downhill, on the left, is a sign for Balcões, a viewpoint you might like to visit later in the day; see pages 64-65). Following the 'Portela' sign, you join the fast-flowing **Levada do Furado**. While this levada can be tricky underfoot and somewhat vertiginous, the stretch we follow on this circuit is fairly tame, so you will have plenty of opportunity to appreciate the play of light and shade created by the laurel and heath trees.

In **20min** you pass a tunnel on the right, where a waterfall feeds the levada. In **1h**, just by a bridge over the **Ribeira do Poço do Bezerro**, two fast-flowing, channelled levadas course down into the main channel at a grassy verge (see photograph overleaf). The finches here have been tamed by decades of walkers using *Landscapes of Madeira*, and will expect to be fed some titbits!

Distance: 7km/4.3mi; 2h50min

Grade: moderate, with an ascent of 300m/1000ft. *Not suitable in wet weather or heavy mist!*

Equipment: walking boots or stout shoes that grip on slippery surfaces, long trousers, warm clothing all year round, water

Transport: 56 or 103 to Ribeiro Frio; 103 to return. Or . Buses stop at the Ribeiro Frio Restaurant; there is a large souvenir shop (and a bar) opposite

Refreshments en route:
Restaurante Ribeiro Frio (start/end)
Bar Ribeiro Frio (start/end)
Bar Flor da Selva (on the Balcões path; optional extension)

Points of interest:
trout hatchery and small botanical gardens
old trails and farm at Feiteiras
Levada do Furado
source of the Levada do Bezerro

Optional extension:
Balcões (2km; 40min return): see pages 64-65

Turn right at the finches ...

The walk described in that book continues along the Furado levada and then down to Portela, but for this circuit, you now head uphill to the right. Clamber 2m/6ft up the bank above the *left-hand* channel, to a path. Follow this beside the narrow **Levada do Bezerro**, rising through ferns and greenery in the setting shown opposite. You come to some lovely pools and polished boulders in the **Ribeira do Poço do Bezerro** (**2h**), where this levada takes its source.

around ribeiro frio **walk 5**

... and follow the narrow Levada do Bezerro up past waterfalls to its source. Then return and climb a sometimes-stepped path to the plateau.

From here retrace your steps for 30m/yds, then turn left up a narrow path. The path takes you up to a plateau (the **Chão das Feiteiras; 2h15min**). Head straight across, northeast, through ferns *(feiteiras)*, aiming for the right-hand side of the col ahead. If the weather is clear, you will quickly spot **three farm buildings** ahead and to the right. If it's foggy, you may not see them until you're virtually at the front door (**2h25min**)!

Turn right on the grassy track in front of the buildings but, after 200m/yds, turn left on a grassy trail, going through a gate after 20m. Soon cobbles come underfoot. Descend to the ER103, cross it, and pick up the continuing trail 200m/yds downhill. When this beautiful old trail again meets the ER103 (**2h35min**), turn right downhill for a couple of minutes, then pick up the continuation of the trail, on the left. Finally you emerge in a

Old trail down to the trout farm (left) and light and shade on the Levada do Furado

beautiful setting, where a levada descends in tiers just above the **trout farm**. Inspect the hatchery (work up an appetite!), take a look at the tiny botanical gardens, then make your way back down to the Restaurante Ribeiro Frio for a late lunch (**2h50min**). It's quite pricey, but the setting is utterly charming.

If you have time after lunch, take a short walk to one of the island's most spectacular viewpoints — **Balcões** (the balconies); it's just 2km; 40min there and back. The wide, signposted path is below the souvenir shop and bar. Follow it beside the *dry* Levada do Furado, past another bar. In 20 minutes you'll pass through a cut in the towering, moss-covered basalt and find

Balcões: view over the Fajã da Nogueira Valley and to the high peaks (from left to right: Pico do Arieiro, the pointed needle of Pico do Gato, the jagged spires of Pico das Torres and finally Pico Ruivo and the Achada do Teixeira plateau)

yourself high in the Metade Valley. Soon come to a fork, where the old levada goes left; turn right and you're at the **Balcões** in a minute. There are superb views over Fajã da Nogueira and to the high peaks. The power station you see below you is where water collected from the north is channelled via the long tunnels of the Levada dos Tornos to the João Gomes Valley, explored on Walk 1.

You can also walk along the old levada *for a short way* (to where a path drops down to the power station road), but beyond this point it's completely crumbled away.

Restaurante Ribeiro Frio

The jury is still out on this one! Originally opened in the early 1980s and called Victor's, this restaurant was one of our favourites. On our last visit, the name had changed (but not the menu). There was no service, despite it being after noon; most people just walked out. Yet we *have* received good reports from correspondents. There is a lovely 'snug' bar, as well as the main restaurant (with simple benches). Do *not* arrive between 09.00-11.30, when the coaches create absolute havoc!

The trout farm (above) and rustic setting of the Restaurante Ribeiro Frio

RESTAURANTE RIBEIRO FRIO
Ribeiro Frio (**575 898**
daily 09.30-18.00 €—€€€

trout (from the fish farm) is the speciality — including thick trout soup, and baked, grilled or smoked trout

soups, **omelettes** and **salads** for a light meal

various **pastas**

fish dishes include tuna steak, *espada* with banana (see *our* recipe on page 29), grilled *bacalhau*

meats include mixed grill, steaks, pork, chicken and, surprisingly, **lamb cutlets**

coffee or tea with a good selection of **cakes** and **tarts** from €

restaurants

eat

Trout soup (sopa de truta)
Despite the Portuguese name, this recipe comes from the Black Forest (Victor was German).

Cook the trout in 4 cups of cold water with the bay, clove and bouquet garni for about 20 minutes. Then put in a blender (or mash down) and heat till reduced to about 3 cups. Add the cream, salt, pepper. Add 1 tbsp. cold water to the egg yolk to prevent curdling, then add a little hot liquid. Return to the pan (do *not* let it boil) and stir as it thickens.

Place the smoked trout bits in warm soup plates and pour over the hot soup. Sprinkle with the freshly chopped dill.

Lamb cutlets (costeleta de borrego)
A popular dish at Easter — a treat, as young lamb does not often figure in the local diet.

Marinate the cutlets in all the other ingredients and refrigerate, covered, overnight. Then grill or barbecue, basting liberally with the marinade. Serve with mashed potato (with garlic and olive oil).

Ingredients (for 4 people)
for the soup:
1 fresh trout, boned, skinned, filleted and cut into small pieces
1/2 smoked trout fillet, cut in slivers
1 bay leaf, 1 clove, 1 bouquet garni, salt and fresh-ground pepper
1 egg yolk
2 cups double cream
fresh dill

for the cutlets
8 lamb cutlets
1 clove garlic, crushed
200 ml white wine
100 ml olive oil
2 cloves, 2 bay leaves
fresh chopped parsley
salt and pepper to taste

recipes

eat

This invigorating hike first takes you high above the sea, with fine views to São Lourenço. You'll cross grassy terraces veined with old stone walls, then take a narrow, often precipitous path down to Caniçal. The second leg follows a narrow levada through delightful woodlands, before making a dramatic descent to the old main road.

caniçal circuit

WALK

Start out at the **Pico do Facho** bus stop on the west side of the **Caniçal tunnel**. Climb the road towards the peak. Electricity pylons will guide you from here to Caniçal: *take note of them!* The **first pylon** comes up just before the peak: you will leave the road here and walk left on a path (almost opposite a trail rising up from Machico). But first walk another five minutes up to **Pico do Facho** (**25min**), for a wonderful view of Machico and its harbour, the airport and São Lourenço Point.

Return to the pylon and, some 10m/yds below it, turn right on the old trail — which may be obscured by tall grass or bits of rubbish initially. Make for the **second pylon**, ahead. Your path passes well above it, at the top of some still-cultivated terraces. It takes you straight to the **third pylon** (**50min**). Here, on a ridge

Distance: 9km/5.6mi; 3h30min

Grade: moderate, with overall ascents/descents of about 300m/ 1000ft; you must be sure-footed and have a head for heights (danger of vertigo).

Equipment: walking boots, sunhat, long-sleeved shirt, long trousers, plenty of water

Transport: 🚌 113 to/from the Caniçal tunnel on the ER109: alight at the western end and return from the eastern end. 🚗 By car, park well tucked in at the side of the road to Pico do Facho (or park at Caniçal and start the walk there — if you can wait 4-5h to eat!).

Shorter version: do either half of the main walk, ending at or starting from the old church in Caniçal (🚌 113). Grade and equipment as above. About 1h30min.

Refreshments en route:
O Tonel, 350m west of where the walk starts, on the ER109
Restaurants/snack bars in Caniçal (halfway point)

Points of interest:
Pico do Facho viewpoint
whaling museum in Caniçal; 10.00-12.00 and 13.00-18.00; closed Mondays and holidays (961 404

between the **Ilhéu** and **Pejal** streams, you enjoy you first views of Caniçal.

Watch out here. The path seems to 'disappear' on bedrock. In fact it unexpectedly turns *inland,* to descend the north side of the ridge. So go *left* up the bedrock and after 20 paces fork right, to continue the descent into the next valley. Soon (**1h**) the **fourth**

Humpback bridge over the Ribeira do Natal

pylon is about 150m/yds ahead of you. *Watch out here, too!* Do *not* follow the path towards this pylon. The path you want (not easily seen at first) turns off to the right and runs about 20m/60ft *below* the pylon and rounds it on the sea side, zigzagging and dropping considerably.

When you come to the next bedrock area at a precipice (**1h05min**), the path bends sharply to the left. You overlook Caniçal here. Ten minutes from this precipice, you pass to the left of the **fifth pylon** (**1h20min**), from where the end of the walk is in view. Looking inland, you spot a beautiful old humpback footbridge over the **Natal** stream below. The path takes you down to it — a scramble involving all fours. Once over the **bridge** (**1h25min**), take the tarmac road down to the seafront. On the far side of the building (bar, toilets), pick up the seafront promenade and follow it along the coast to **Caniçal**. Turn left uphill in the centre — the **whaling museum** will be on your right. (Or first walk a little further along the front, to Bar/Restaurante Amarelo on the left.)

Continue uphill to the **old church** (**1h40min**; bus stop). Head east from the church on the main street, then take the second left turn; Caniçal's large **newer church** (with a clock) is on the right. When you meet the ER109 to Abra Bay (**2h**), cross straight over, passing to the left of the 'Correos' building. *(Or first have lunch at Restaurante Jardim — 300m to the left, on the street to the left.)* Climb the road at the left of the 'Correos'; a green wire fence is to your right. The road reverts to track and makes for the wood ahead. Over to the right, volcanic rock in hues of reds, yellows, golds and greens catches the eye.

Keep beside the gutter at the left of the road; it leads you to the narrow **Levada do Caniçal**, which soon enters a **wood** full of mimosas (**2h20min**). Follow this small levada as it curves left, away from the track (which continues straight on). Soon you pass a **narrower levada** rushing down to the left (**2h30min**). Then, from a grassy verge, you have a splendid view down to Caniçal and towards the wind generators on São Lourenço Point.

The same view comes into focus 20 minutes later, this time from the far side of the **Ribeira do Serrado** (see photograph page 68). Three minutes later you can avoid the awkward levada bridge by using the path in the stream bed below (**2h55min**). Before long the fine buttress of rock formed by the **Lombo do Vento** and **Pico Judeu** rises nearby on your right.

Dramatic end of the walk, high above the ER109, with Caniçal below in the distance

A red earthen track crosses the levada, and you leave the woods behind. With more wide-ranging views, you near the end of the walk. The levada rounds a bend and now the narrow path runs at the top of a concrete wall high above the ER109 ... and below a quarry (**3h15min**). This is a stunning section of the hike. When you come to a concrete track, descend left to the road, where you can *flag down* a bus (**3h20min**). Motorists should turn right and follow the road through the **Caniçal road tunnel** (add 15min; there is a pavement, but this is still very unpleasant — it's almost worth taking a bus to the far side!).

Restaurante Jardim

As is name implies, this restaurant is set in lovely gardens. You can dine indoors (huge windows) or on the outdoor terrace with retractable roof. Beautifully decorated, spotlessly maintained, this is an extremely pleasant atmosphere for enjoying a meal.

JARDIM
Sítio Palmeira de Baixo,
Caniçal (969 120
daily except Mon 10.00-
23.00 €–€€

large selection of **entrées**, specialising in all kinds of shellfish, octopus, etc

soups and **omelettes** for a lighter meal

fish dishes include tuna steak, *espada* (fillets or on the bone), sauteed octopus with chips, *bacalhau*, creamed mixed shellfish

meats steak with mush-rooms, pork cutlets, *picado* (sautéed meat and chips)

basic **sweets** — including the ubiquitous velvet *pudim* and chocolate mousse

reasonable **wine list**, mostly Alentejos

Jardim, with views to the outdoor terrace

Another, newer restaurant that we have not tried is **Bar/Restaurante Amarelo** (961 798) on the promenade (but it was even recommended at Jardim, so is probably good). **O Tonel**, 350 m west of the Pico do Facho road (open daily 10.00-22.00, (962 459), has been around since time immemorial and serves very standard Madeiran fare in an old-fashioned setting.

restaurants

eat

Steak with mushrooms (bife com cogumelos)

Quickly fry the steaks in hot oil just until brown on both sides and very rare inside; set aside. Lower the heat and add the shallots and mushrooms to the pan; sauté for about 3-4 minutes; set aside.

Add the brandy or madeira to the pan and use a match to burn off the alcohol. When the flame subsides, add the broth, stirring, then cream to taste. Stirring, reduce the sauce to half. Return the beef and mushrooms to the pan; reheat and season.

Chocolate mousse (mousse de chocolate)

Melt the chocolate in a double boiler, then let cool. Gently whisk together the egg yolks. When the chocolate is cool, stir in the yolks.

Beat the whites to form soft peaks, then slowly add the sugar. Using a metal spoon, gently fold the whites into the chocolate until thoroughly mixed. Spoon into serving dishes and refrigerate, covered, for at least an hour.

Ingredients (for 4 people)

for the steak
4 sirloin or fillet steaks
2 tbsp olive oil
175 g button mushrooms
2 tsp chopped shallots
4 tbsp brandy or madeira wine
4 tbsp cream (or to taste)
150 ml beef broth or bouillon
salt and pepper to taste

for the mousse
200 g dark chocolate (75% cocoa or higher), in small pieces
3 large eggs, separated
40 g caster sugar

recipes

eat

This easy (but quite long) walk in the Serra das Funduras takes you through an area where the ancient *laurisilva* forest is being regenerated with the help of EU funding. You'll walk among not only laurels, but *folhados* (see Walk 10), myrtles and tree ferns.

serra das funduras

WALK

Begin the walk at **Portela**: head east on the narrow road skirting the north side of the restaurant **Miradouro da Portela**. The narrow **Levada da Portela** runs along on your right. When the tarred road swings right (to Ribeira de Machico), keep ahead on an earthen track. After 200m/yds you pass an old trail down left to Porto da Cruz. In the 1800s the *borracheiros* used this trail to transport wine, carried in goatskins, from Porto da Cruz to the south. There are magnificent views down over 'Eagle Rock' and the north coast … *if* the weather is fine.

At a fork (**20min**), keep left (Portela's transmitter mast is up to the right). You come to the first of several '**Serra das Funduras**' information panels (**27min**), showing the various routes in these hills. Distances for each of the segments are shown, too, which will help you shorten the walk if you like. From this sign, turn right on the first of the three footpaths created in the forest; this one is 2.5km long. While dense foliage obscures most of the views, there are occasional glimpses of the Machico Valley and

Distance: 16km/10mi; 3h55min

Grade: easy, but quite long (ample opportunities to shorten the walk; see the map on page 79). If the weather is poor, keep to the footpaths; the tracks are quite boring, unless the views are fine! Some of the paths are narrow and slippery; you must be sure-footed.

Equipment: stout shoes, warm clothing all year round, sunhat, plenty of water and snacks

Transport: 🚌 53 or 78 to/from Portela, or by 🚗

Refreshments en route:
Bar/Restaurant Miradouro da Portela at the viewpoint; *recommended*
Bar Portela a Vista, below the pass on the Machico road

Points of interest:
laurisilva forest (under protection)
views to Penha de Águia and over the north coast

In the *laurisilva* (left) and steps opposite the forestry house

the golf course at Santo da Serra. The path undulates along the contours, just on the leeward side of the ridge.

Eventually steps on the left take you back to the track (**1h10min**). Turn right and come almost at once to another **signboard**. On the left are picnic tables and the second footpath. We will return by that path; for now, follow the track downhill to the right. Three minutes later, at a junction, go left. In another seven minutes, go left again at another junction, descending slightly. You round the huge basin of the **Ribeira das Cales**. At

a fork, keep left uphill, to the **Casa das Funduras** (forestry house), opened in 2002 (**1h45min**). There are more picnic tables here.

Leaving the forestry house off to the right, stay on the track which curls left. *Ignore* a path on the right 200m/yds along but, 25m further on, fork right on the third sign-posted footpath (1km). When it ends, more steps take you up left to another picnic area and **viewpoint** (**1h55min**), from where Pico do Facho is seen. From here go left along the track, passing the EU-sponsors' signboard on your left.

Back at the forestry house (**2h 05min**), climb the path on your right. This rises above the track, with fine views to conical **Pico Coroa** at the head of the valley. This path (also 2.5km) is perhaps the prettiest of all, dotted with fern trees.

Restaurante Miradouro da Portela (the original cottage has the thatched roof) and the deep wood fire in the snug, where espetada sizzles

When you meet the track again (**2h45min**) go right, uphill (or, if visibilty is poor, keep to the prettier path). Once over a rise, 15 minutes along the track, you regain fine views over the north coast. Follow the track all the way back to **Portela** (**3h55min**). We do hope you've worked up an appetite!

Miradouro da Portela

We'll never forget our first meal here. We'd been walking the Levada do Furado (see Walk 5) from Ribeiro Frio to Portela on a cold, miserable day. Our only sustenance was some 'Reid's Cake' (see page 36-37) which we'd scoffed in the shelter of rock overhangs. Eventually descending to Portela in drizzle, a thatched cottage (as it was then) loomed ahead in the fog. Inside was a rip-roaring fire. Bliss!

MIRADOURO DA PORTELA
Portela (966 169
daily 09.30-22.00 €

espetada is the speciality, but there are **soups** and **omelettes**, including parsley *(salsa)* omlette, for a lighter meal

We were famished. They suggested their 'usual' menu, which turned out to be the marathon meal described on the next two pages! Luckily we had until early evening to catch the last bus back to Funchal. It was delicious — one of the most memorable meals we've ever had on the island.

Now, forewarned, we only order *one espetada* for two people (pictured above is *one* serving — 6 large cubes). The wood fire is so hot that *espetada* of fillet (this is the *only* restaurant we know that offers a *choice of beef*) cooks in three minutes. With a bottle of red Quinta do Monte, it is superb. They *do* have a large restaurant room, but we always opt for the cosy snug, with its hard wooden benches.

restaurants

eat

THE 'WHOLE WORKS'

Tomato soup *(sopa de tomate)*

Simmer the tomatoes, potatoes and onion together in the oil for 15 minutes or so, until very soft. (If you use tinned tomatoes, you'll need *three* 400 g tins to retain enough liquid.) Then purée (or sievel; season to taste. Serve with a poached egg on top. (See photograph on page 92, which shows this soup in a different style — the onions have not been puréed; at the Miradouro da Portela they *are*.)

Flat bread *(bolo do caco)*

Mix all the ingredients together, using enough water to make a light, puffy dough. Allow to rise, then knead well on a floured board until it has an elastic consistency. Cover and leave to rise for another hour.

Divide and mould into four circles. Unless you have a wood-burning oven (in which case cook them on a hot stonel, fry like pancakes on a very hot non-stick griddle, turning after they have spread to about 3 cm thick and the first side has a fine crust. Serve hot with butter or garlic butter. (See photograph on page 7.)

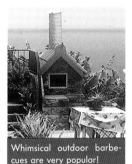
Whimsical outdoor barbecues are very popular!

Ingredients (for 4 people)

for the soup:
1 kg tomatoes, peeled and chopped
2 small onions, finely chopped
2 medium potatoes, cubed
garlic juice to taste (optional)
4 eggs
2 tbsp olive oil
salt and pepper

for the bread
1 kg plain flour
1 kg puréed sweet potatoes, cooled
25 g yeast
warm salted water as needed
salt to taste

recipes

eat

Beef on a skewer *(espetada)*

Roll the beef cubes in the crushed garlic and salt and let it 'rest' for half an hour. Put on skewers or laurel branches, inserting a fresh laurel (bay) leaf between each cube. Cook over a hot fire, preferably with some laurel twigs in the wood or charcoal. In this photo, taken at our barbecue in Funchal, the potatoes (in foil) baked in 30 minutes; the (fillet) of beef was done (rare) in 10 minutes.

'Oven chips'

Preheat the oven to 180°C, 350°F, gas mark 4. Chop the potatoes into 3 cm cubes and boil in salted water for 5 minutes, then drain well and dry off in the warm cooking pan for another 5 minutes.

Transfer to an oven pan lightly coated with olive oil. Sprinkle with a little coarse salt and some finely-crushed dry laurel leaves. Toss the lot together with wooden spoons and roast, turning a couple of times, for 30 about minutes.

<u>Ingredients (for 4 people)</u>

2 kg of sirloin or fillet steak, cut into 5 cm cubes (if you are using a tougher cut of beef, first marinate it in white wine for 24 hours)

6 garlic cloves, crushed

coarse salt (to taste)

laurel twigs and plenty of fresh bay leaves

4 large potatoes (if baking), or 8 medium potatoes, peeled (if making 'oven chips')

olive oil

salad makings, salad dressing

An old zigzag trail, high cliffs, the throbbing sea beside you … this walk was made in heaven. The ideal way to do it is to take bus 56 or 103 to *Santana*, see the village, then *walk* 2km to the Quinta do Furão for lunch (at 12 sharp!). Unless you have a car, end at São Jorge or take the short-cut path to the Vigia, to catch the last bus!

santana and são jorge

WALK

To start the walk, climb the cobbled road on the north side of the **'Solar' bus stop**, passing flower-filled gardens. In **4min** you come to a rosy-pink *solar,* now in ruins. These early manors were the homes of sugar-mill and plantation owners. Fork right in front of the entrance, curving below the building on a cobbled trail, overlooking the **Achada do Gramacho**, a small plain laced with vines.

On reaching a tarred road at the **Quinta do Furão**, turn left and walk up 10m/yds, to where 'Stop' is written on the road, then turn right. (Or first have lunch at the Quinta!) Follow this road for some 700m/0.5mi; it skirts to the west of a conical hill, the **Cabeço da Vigia**. Just before you reach the highest point in the road, where there is a stand of pines on the left and a blue sign, 'São Jorge, Calhau',

Distance: 10.5km/6.5mi; 3h30min

Grade: moderate-strenuous, with over 400m/1300ft of descents/ ascents. *Not recommended in damp weather, when the trails would be slippery, or in strong winds.*

Equipment: walking boots, warm clothing, long trousers, swimwear, sunhat, snacks, water

Transport: 🚌 103 or 138 (Arco bus). Ask for **'Vail**-yoh So-**lahr'** (the old *solar*); the stop is 1.7km northwest of Santana's town hall (150m north of Bragados Restaurant), 400m south of the Quinta do Furão road. Or 🚌 56 to Santana. Return on 🚌 103 from the Vigia turn-off at São Jorge; *be there at least 10min before departure time from São Jorge.* By 🚗: park in São Jorge or at the Vigia and take 🚌 103 or 138 *east* to the start.

Shorter walk: Santana — São Jorge. 7.5km/4.7mi; 2h37min. End the walk at São Jorge's church.

Refreshments en route:
Bragados restaurant (near the start)
Quinta do Furão (see pages 90-91)
bar/café at Calhau bathing area
bar in São Jorge

Points of interest:
Santana village
São Jorge's baroque church
old port of Calhau/bathing area

go left down an earthen track. Soon the old cobbled trail shown on page 84 is visible beneath the iron-rich soil. You've begun the exhilarating descent into the **Ribeira de São Jorge**. The setting is magnificent: the great peaks rise inland while, ahead of you, São Jorge's church and lighthouse glimmer brightly above a blue, blue sea. On the far side of the valley, you can see your old cobbled trail up to São Jorge. Another path skirts the coast.

All too soon the descent ends; at **1h** you're crossing the old bridge by a new bathing area. Turn right and follow the coastal path*, past a beautifully kept house beside the banana groves. Just beyond it are the few remains of **Calhau**, once such an important port that it boasted both a church *and* a chapel! Part of an old wall, with remnants of tiles, still rises near the sea. Opposite the first of the ruins is a **tap** and the trail we'll climb later to São Jorge. The wide sea-side path takes you deliciously close to the pounding breakers. You

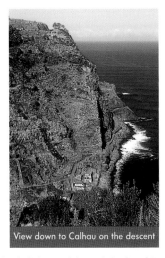

View down to Calhau on the descent

come to a deep inlet just below the lighthouse (**1h20min**); ahead is a fishermen's bridge over to the **Ponta de São Jorge**. This bridge is often damaged by rock falls; enjoy the view *from a distance!* If you are pressed for time, you can climb the old trail from here straight up to the Vigia; then, if time allows, walk on to São Jorge's church and catch the bus there.

Return to Calhau (**1h40min**), then go up the steep trail by the tap. As you climb, look across to your descending trail, etched into the cliff on the far side of the river. By **2h15min** you will have huffed and puffed up to a junction. Cross half-left over the

*A new bathing complex is being built here. No doubt it will have a bar/café, but it was impossible to tell at time of writing how this will affect the landscape, or whether the photograph above will be out-of-date.

road and climb cobbled steps towards the cream-coloured walls of São Jorge's cemetery. Facing the **cemetery gate** (**2h25min**), turn right up a road, after seven minutes passing to the right of the chapel shown here. Continue round left to visit the magnificent baroque church in the centre of **São Jorge** (**2h37min**). Nearby are a bar and a bus stop.

Walk back to the palm-shaded chapel and turn left. Ignore a road off right; continue ahead along the **Estrada Municipal do Farrobo.** Beyond a stream (**Corrego do Farrobo**), climb to a T-junction and turn right to visit the **lighthouse** (**3h**). Then return to the *estrada municipal* and turn right. At a three-way junction turn right to the **Vigia** ('look-out', once used by whalers; **3h25min**). From here the views west capture the attention, especially over Ponta Delgada's seaside church on a flat spit of land and the huge hotel, with Cabanas above and Ribeira da Janela in the distance.

Return to the Estrada Municipal do Farrobo (**3h30min**) — you can flag down a bus at the 'Vigia' signpost. (*Arrive 10 minutes early, to be on the safe side!*)

The little chapel at São Jorge and the interior of the baroque church; left: maize drying on an old Santana house

Quinta do Furão

No doubt the best time of year to visit this five-star hotel is during the grape harvest in the autumn (when guests are encouraged to join in the grape pressing and ensuing festivities), but it's gorgeous all year round. And you needn't expect to pay five-star prices if you just visit for a light lunch as described overleaf (or snack at the pub which opens an hour later).

Moreover, the menu boasts many regional specialities. We

Old wine press (above) and vine-yards at the Quinta do Furão

restaurants

eat

QUINTA DO FURÃO
Achada do Gramacho, Santana
(570 100/101/102
www.quintadofurao.com
restaurant open daily, 12.00-15.30
and 19.00-21.30 €–€€€; pub 13.00-
22.00 €

huge menu, as befits a 5-star hotel

Specialities include

entrées: fish soup with celery and
saffron, tomato and onion soup,
limpets (see over), tomato and fresh
Santana cheese in balsamic vinegar

fish: espada fillets with almonds or
with banana and 'madeira' sauce
(the latter being a combination of
white wine, sercial, butter and
garlic)

meat: bife à Caldeirão Verde (fillet
steak done like beef Wellington, but
with Roquefort cheese), espetada

While you wait: pickled tripe, pigs'
ears and tuna ...

were pleasantly astounded, on
our first visit, to be presented
with the tray of nibblers shown
above — titbits more likely to
appeal to a Madeiran palate than
an international clientèle! (These
free hors d'oeuvres vary day by day.) Naturally there is a very
extensive wine list (the hotel is owned by the Madeira Wine
Company); the Porta da Ravessa (an Alentejo) was dry and fragrant
— a perfect accompaniment to our lunch of soup and grilled limpets.

There are quite a few other restaurants in Santana. One of the
oldest is at the hotel **O Colmo**, where in the past we have dined on
a most memorable crayfish stew. Nowadays Colmo is usually
inundated with tourist coaches. Coaches also call at the Furão three
days a week (days vary), so arrive at noon sharp! If it's a fine day, no
doubt you'll want to lunch outdoors on the lovely terrace.

LIGHT LUNCH AT QUINTA DO FURÃO

Tomato soup and country or 'house' bread (pão da casa)

The tomato soup recipe is on page 82 but note, in the photogaph below, that the Furão leaves the onions in fine slices, *not* puréed.

For the bread, knead the starter dough, then knead in the potato purée and finally the flour. Add warm water as necessary to achieve an elastic consistency.

Cover and leave to rise overnight. Mould into an oblong loaf and cook in a hot oven (230°C, 450°F, gas mark 8) for 30 minutes (or until it sounds hollow when tapped).

Grilled limpets (lapas grelhadas)

Arrange the limpets on clean shells in a cast iron pan (as above) or any suitable grilling tray. Pour over the butter, lemon and garlic juice, and grill for just three minutes. Serve with 'country bread'.

Ingredients (for 4 people)
for the country bread
1 kg plain flour
200 g sweet potatoes, puréed
100 g starter dough (5 g yeast, 100 g flour, warm water, salt)
for the limpets
4 dozen limpets and clean limpet shells
150 melted butter
juice of one lemon
4 lemons (for serving)
garlic juice to taste

MEMORIES OF COLMO

We've no idea how the memorable crayfish stew was done at O Colmo many years ago, or whether they still make it. But this is a very easy recipe to make with limited cooking facilities when you are on Madeira — or to enjoy back home — *if* you can buy *really fresh* crayfish or lobster.

Crayfish stew
(caldeirada de langostins)

Melt the butter in a flameproof casserole or heavy-bottomed frying pan and then add the chopped onion and sliced carrot. Cover and simmer over a low heat for 10 minutes.

Stir in the mustard and add the crayfish (or shrimp). Pour over the cream and port or madeira; recover. Simmer gently over a low heat for about 15 minutes, until the shellfish is cooked.

Serve with boiled rice or boiled potatoes, 'country bread' and a green salad. Fabulous!

Ingredients (for 4 people)

1.5 kg uncooked crayfish, in the shells, but cleaned and slit open

110 g unsalted butter

1 small onion, finely chopped

1/2 carrot, finely sliced

1 tbsp Dijon mustard

200 ml double cream

200 ml red port wine or madeira wine

recipes

eat

Like Walks 3, 5, 8 and 13, this route follows a restored old zigzag trail — in this case one that clings precariously to a sugar-loaf cliff. From a distance the route looks impossible — and indeed it was for most people before the railings were built. Today the easy route lets you relax and savour the tremendous coastal views.

caminho da entrosa

WALK

The walk begins at the **church** in **Boaventura**: head southeast along the ER101 towards Santana. Continue along the road for 300m/yds, then turn left in front of the electricity substation, passing the **Solar de Boaventura** (see page 97) on your left.

Some 1.2km down this road, descend the path on the right, the '**Camino do Calhau**' (**20min**). After crossing the **Ribeira do Porco** on a stone bridge, it's worth exploring the picturesque old **ruins** to the left, above the mouth of the river. To reach them, either take the narrow path on the left through a red clay gully (an awkward scramble at the outset; the path is shown overleaf) or bear right on the main

Distance: 6.5km/ 4mi; 2h50min

Grade: moderate ups and downs of 370m/1220ft overall. You must be sure-footed, but there is no danger of vertigo.

Equipment: stout shoes or walking boots, warm clothing, sunhat, water, walking stick; swimwear in summer

Transport: 🚌 6 or 🚗 to/from Boaventura (motorists can shorten a return walk by 3km/45min by parking at the Caminho do Calhau; see car symbol on the map). Or do as a one-way walk, ending at Arco and returning on 🚌 103 (quite easy, with an ascent of just 180m).

Refreshments en route:
Solar de Boaventura near the start of the walk (see page 97)
Snack Bar/Restaurante Arco (the halfway point or end; see page 97)

Points of interest:
beautiful old trail
ruined mill
mini-museum at the Solar

path and, at a fork by another stone ruin, turn left. *We* think the ruins are the remains of an old textile mill: our Madeiran history book refers to such ruins in this area, where 'fabric was made using the red clay obtained nearby'. But the locals, who haven't read our history book, seem convinced it was a sugar-mill (admittedly very common around here).

Red clay gully in the Ribeira do Porco

From the lone ruin the beautiful old trail (**Caminho da Entrosa**) rises in easy zigzags round the vertical cliff. The views straight down to the sea are breathtaking, but very sturdy railings ensure no danger of vertigo. Historians (who were probably carried round the sugar-loaf in hammocks) also marvelled at the huge house leeks on these cliffs — 'the size of hats'.

The trail emerges at the **Snack Bar/Restaurante Arco** on the ER101 (**1h20min**; bus 6, 103, 132). After a break for refreshment, return the same way to **Boaventura** (**2h50min**).

Solar de Boaventura

Once a private manor house, then a school, then the health centre, this *solar* opened as an hotel in 1992 and expanded in 1998. Lovely public rooms with comfy sofas ranged round a mini-museum of artefacts — from an old loom and still to old telephones; cozy bar; gardens; two dining rooms — in the old house, with open fire, or the newer conservatory (without shades — beware, it can be *very* hot!).

SOLAR DE BOAVENTURA
Boaventura (860 888
daily lunch and dinner €–€€€

ten **entrées**, including 'Entrada Solar' (swordfish, salmon, plain and smoked ham, egg, mixed shellfish, sardines, mayonnaise, cucumber, tomato and lettuce!)

soups and **omelettes**; **spaghetti**

fish *espada* (see page 99), sole, tuna, mixed grill, shellfish with rice or spaghetti

meats include steak, lamb chops, some imaginative pork dishes (including pork with fruit and curry), chicken

good selection of **cakes** and **tarts** — with or without **home-made ice cream**

SNACK BAR/RESTAURANTE ARCO
Arco de São Jorge, ER 101 (no (available)
daily, all day €

soups and **sandwiches**

fish *espada*, octopus, parrot fish *(bobião)*

meats include steak, lamb or pork chops, beef stew with vegetables *(jardineira)*, chicken

---

Solar da Boaventura and the loom in the museum; below: Snack Bar/Restaurante Arco

restaurants

eat

SOLAR SPECIALITIES

Pork escalopes *(escalopes de porco)*

Season the pork escalopes with the crushed garlic, salt and pepper. Dust lightly with flour and gently fry in olive oil on a low heat, turning once, until golden.

Remove the escalopes from the pan, transfer to a warm plate and keep warm in the oven. Now use the same pan to make the sauce. Add the white wine and lemon juice and simmer this mixture until it reduces to make a syrupy sauce.

Pour the sauce over the meat and serve with boiled potatoes and vegetables — in the case of the Solar, three or four different vegetables in season!

<u>Ingredients (for 4 people)</u>
8 pork escalopes (about 800 g)
200 ml white wine
garlic, crushed, to taste
flour for dusting
olive oil
juice of 2 lemons
salt and pepper

recipes

eat

Espada pigalli (not shown)

Bring enough water to cover the fillets to a gentle boil; add the salt, pepper, garlic and parsley. Poach over a gentle heat for about 6-7 minutes. Keep warm.

For the sauce, use 200 ml of the cooking water and add the white wine, Pernod and cream. Simmer till it reduces to a smooth sauce.

'Filled' *espada* (*espada recheada*)

Immerse the fillets in the wine for 15min, then remove; set aside the wine. Season the fish with garlic, salt and pepper. Then dust with flour and fry in 1 tbsp olive oil for 6-7 minutes. Keep warm.

Make a sauce by gently warming the cream, mayonnaise and remaining wine; let thicken, add the prawns and simmer for a further couple of minutes. Pour over the fish.

Ingredients for both recipes (for 4 people)

8 fillets of *espada* (about 650 g)
200 ml white wine
garlic, crushed, to taste
salt and pepper

Ingredients for the individual recipes (for 4 people)

for the pigalli:
4 shot glasses of Pernod
2 tbsp fresh chopped parsley
100 g double cream

for the filled espada
200 g pre-cooked prawns
100 ml double cream
100 g mayonnaise

Power and majesty. These may be your first impressions of the Levada do Norte. You are at the centre of the north/south cleft that splits the island. The high peaks rise in the east; the magnificent valley of Serra de Água lies to the south. At your feet, 1.5m deep and just as wide, the levada surges along in a massive channel.

folhadal

WALK

Start the walk opposite the **Bar/Restaurante Encumeada**, on the south side of Encumeada Pass, where a sign indicates 'Folhadal'. Climb the concrete steps up to the **Levada do Norte** and follow it westwards, past the keepers' flower-filled house. You'll be amazed by the abundance of vegetation: conifers of every description, heath and hawthorn, with a tangle of laurel, azaleas, lilies, hydrangeas, and myriad wild flowers. If you're walking here in June, you'll see the splendid cornflower-blue 'Pride of Madeira' in all its glory.

In **12min** you come to the promontory of **Lapa do Galho**: from here you enjoy fine views down over the valley and the south coast. You can also see the levada continuing to the east and emptying into the metal pipe down to the Serra de Água

Distance: 8.5km/5.3mi; 2h50min

Grade: easy, but you must be sure-footed and have a head for heights (**danger of vertigo** on the Levada das Rabaças). Two tunnels (one fairly long).

Equipment: stout shoes, **good torch for each member of the party**, warm clothing, sunhat, water

Transport: 🚌 6 or 139 to Encumeada Pass (*not* the Residencial Encumeada). Return on 🚌 6. Or by 🚗: park at the viewpoint on the north side of the pass.

Short walk: Encumeada — Folhadal — Encumeada. 4km/2.5mi; 1h. Equipment, access/return as above. Follow the main walk to Folhadal and back. *A 5-star walk on a fine day*; the paths are amply wide, and there is little danger of vertigo, but *good* torches are essential.

Refreshments en route:
Bar/Restaurante Encumeada (at the start)
Residencial Encumeada (1km south)
Pousada dos Vinháticos (3.5km south); *highly recommended*

Points of interest:
Levada do Norte and its tunnels
laurisilva
folhados (lily-of-the-valley trees)

power station (inaugurated in 1953). There are 50km/ 31mi of channels north of here (including 11km/6.8mi of tunnels). From the power station the water flows on in another 35km/22mi of channels (7km/4.5mi of tunnels) to irrigate the terraces of Ribeira Brava and Câmara de Lobos (see Walk 11, which follows a short stretch of the same levada before making for Cabo Girão).

Past the promontory the levada forks (**14min**). Turn right and follow the Levada do Norte into the **tunnel**, which will take about 10-12 minutes to pass through. We'll never forget our first walk here: we approached the tunnel to find what looked like a washing machine gone mad. Thick white 'foam' was pouring out. It was fog, rushing through from the other side (as it often does: see the photograph on page 100)!

The tunnel exit (**25min**) frames your first glimpse of **Folhadal**, a 'museum' of ferns and indigenous trees — *vinháticos* (madeiran mahogany), *til* trees (laurels) and white-barked *paus brancos* (olive family). But

Left: a *folhado*, the lily-of-the-valley tree native to Madeira. Above: on the levada to Folhadal

your eyes will be drawn to the *folhados* for which this wood is named — the summer-flowering lily-of-the-valley trees, native only to Madeira. Keep ahead through the ancient *laurisilva*, enjoying views to the São Vicente Valley — until you come to a **second tunnel** (**45min**).*

End the Folhadal route here and return the same way to the levada fork (**1h15min**). Now turn right to follow the narrower **Levada das Rabaças** (1970), a 'tributary' of the Levada do

---

*If you don't suffer from vertigo, have a *very good* torch — and plenty of time, you could follow the levada through this and two more tunnels, to a pretty waterhouse above the São Vicente Valley; allow 2h return (50min in tunnels). This is a wonderful, adventurous route through ancient woodlands, but there is no protective fencing.

Norte. It is flowing in from Cascalho, an enormous basin pouring with waterfalls in the upper Ponta do Sol Valley — just one of the sources for this levada. In **1h45min** a **waterfall** on the right heralds a short **tunnel** (three minutes to pass). Seven minutes later, you reach a keepers' lonely house above the Pousada dos Vinháticos. In **2h** you come to a very long **tunnel** which eventually leads to Cascalho.

Turn back here, to the 'Folhadal' sign at **Encumeada** (**2h50min**), where the bus stops.

Vinháticos (top), Restaurante/Snack Bar Encumeada (left), Residencial Encumeada (right)

You have three good choices for lunch near the pass. The nearest is the **Snack Bar/Restaurante Encumeada** across the road. This is a simple, but very pleasant place, with a surprisingly ambitious menu.

Just 1km downhill is the beautifully sited **Residencial Encumeada**, with wide terraces, snack bar, and large dining room. A few guide books wax lyrical about the place and the hearty mountain fare. We've often stopped for a drink, but have been unlucky in our attempts to have a meal … or, indeed, even to get them to send a menu for this book!

Another 2.5km downhill is the **Pousada dos Vinháticos**. It's been one of our favourite places to stay for decades, our little piece of heaven (see over).

**SNACK BAR/RESTAURANTE
ENCUMEADA**
(952 319
daily 08.30-22.00 €

entrées: vegetable or bread soup (açorda), giant prawns, grilled limpets

fish: espada, bacalhau

wide range of **omelettes**

meats: parrilla Argentina (a mixed grill), espetada on laurel skewers, bife a Portuguesa (steak with white wine, garlic and smoked ham), pork cutlet, picado (sautéed meat), feijoada (Brazilian bean stew; 24h notice required)

restaurants

eat

POUSADA DOS VINHATICOS

The *pousada* (the only one on the island) offers *three* separate menus — regional, Portuguese and international. There are also flambés. Try to spend a night: there are just three enchanting rooms in the old house, also an annexe and a newer 'log cabin'! Wake to the sight of Crista do Galo, the beautiful 'cock's comb' ridge behind the building, and to the cheerful breakfast buffet (shown left).

The dining room, set for breakfast (top), and octopus salad

POUSADA DOS VINHATICOS
ER228 above Serra de Água (**952 344**
daily 12.30-21.30 €€-€€€

Selections from the *regional menu:*

a dozen **entrées**, ranging from smoked ham with seasonal fruit, octopus salad (see left), fried banana with bacon and five kinds of home-made soup

fish dishes are confined to e*spada*, *bacalhau* and tuna, but with a variety of sauces

meat dishes are outstanding for those tired of the usual fare. Of course there is *espetada*, but also roast pork loin with chestnuts, braised tongue, rabbit in wine, beef *pousada*-style (with mushrooms; see also recipe on page 75)

very wide selection of **sweets** and excellent **wine list**

Braised ox tongue
(lingua de vaca estufada)

This is *not* the *pousada's* recipe (which is pictured right). It's just a dish we've been making over the years, using madeira wine. By the way, the sliced green vegetable is *pimpinela*, available in the supermarkets. Cook it like squash.

Cover the tongue with cold water. Add the bay leaf and onion. Bring to the boil, skim off any scum that rises to the top, then turn down the heat and cook gently until it reaches the consistency you like — perhaps 3 hours for slightly chewy, 4 hours for melt in the mouth. Drain and keep warm.

For the sauce, take 100 ml of the water the tongue cooked in, add the wine and madeira wine, crushed garlic, cream and seasoning. Simmer, stirring, to reduce, until you have a shiny glazed sauce. Remove the skin from the tongue, slice it, and pour the sauce over. At its best with *garlic mash!*

Ingredients (for 4 people)
1.5 kg ox tongue
200 ml white wine
100 ml madeira wine
100 ml double cream
100 ml water from the cooked meat
2 cloves of garlic, crushed
1 bay leaf
small onion, peeled and stuck with 2 cloves
salt and pepper to taste

recipes

eat

This walk begins in a valley full of cherry trees before progressing above the island's most important vineyard terraces and moving on to the world-famous sea-cliff, Cabo Girão. If you're intrigued (not terrified) by the photograph on the front cover, you can swoop down to the coast in a cable car just west of Câmara de Lobos.

cabo girão

WALK

When the 96 bus roars up the hill at **Estreito**, you'll first pass the church and then a chapel on the left. Just round the next bend is the bus stop, called 'Levada (do Norte)'. **The walk starts** here, on the west side of the road, where you take a paved path under photogenic vine-bearing trellises. The levada is hidden under concrete at first. You'll hear it singing underfoot and soon reach the end of the covered walkway.

At about **20min**, just as the levada bends right into the narrow **Ribeira da Caixa**, *watch for two separate paths down left, a few minutes apart; these avoid awkward, narrow ledges with over-hanging rock*. Soon you'll find yourself deep in the valley; in May it is smothered in cherry blossoms; by early June piles of fruit will be for sale by the roadsides. You cross a tributary and then the main river (**45min**) on levada bridges.

On leaving the valley, the church at **Garachico** comes ino

Distance: 12km/7.5mi; 4h05min

Grade: moderate; a few narrow stretches on the levada demand a head for heights. Little ascent. Overall descents of about 650m/2130ft

Equipment: stout lace-up shoes or walking boots, sunhat, warm clothing in cool weather, water

Transport: 🚌 96 to the levada crossing, 0.7km north of the church at Estreito de Câmara de Lobos; ask for the 'Levada do Norte' bus stop. Return on any bus from the main road at Câmara de Lobos.

Short walk: end the walk at **Cabo Girão** and return on 🚌 154; 7.5km/4.7mi; 2h30min

Refreshments en route:
Bar (after 1h05min)
Snack bar at the cable car (3h15min)
Bars and restaurants at Câmara de Lobos (end of the walk)

Points of interest:
Levada do Norte
vineyard terraces
Cabo Girão
Fajã das Bebras cable car
Câmara de Lobos village

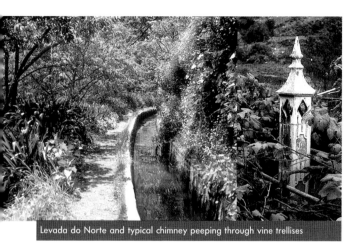

Levada do Norte and typical chimney peeping through vine trellises

view below (**1h05min**; photograph page 108). Five minutes later, climb steps to a road (where a **bar** is advertised up to the right); the levada is on the far side, 25m/yds downhill. At **Nogueira**, the levada seems to end at a brightly-painted house (**1h35min**). Descend the concrete ramp/steps on the left and, when you meet a cobbled road, climb it to regain the channel. Soon a stabilised path takes you over a landslide caused when the factory up to your right collapsed in 1999. Cross the ER229 (**1h45min**) and take steps back down to the levada.

At **Cruz da Caldeira** (**1h58min**), the levada curls right, through a tunnel under Cabo Girão. *Keep ahead here,* alongside a narrow levada. Pass a steeply-stepped path down left and, 10 minutes later, *crossing* steps (you will descend these steps later). Past an overgrown **ruin** (**2h15min**), turn right on a road. Follow this

Cabo Girão and path from the cliff down towards Câmara de Lobos

500m/yds uphill, to the breathtaking **Cabo Girão** viewpoint (**2h30min**).

From the cliff head back down the road. Five minutes down, on a bend to the right, take the steps down to the left (by a small parking bay). Recross the narrow levada, following street lights. When you meet the road lower down, go left. The road ends at a **turning circle** (**2h50min**). Continue straight ahead on the concrete path/steps shown above. In under 10 minutes you meet another road. Follow this to the right, to the end of the promontory at **Rancho**, where a **cable car** (**3h15min**) runs down to **Fajã das Bebras**, a landslip just east of the one shown on the cover. From the promontory more wide steps (the **Caminho Velho do Rancho)** take you back down to the road. Now follow the road to the right. At a Y-fork (**4h50min**), keep left. You will pass a turn-off to the expressway and ten minutes later come into **Câmara de Lobos** (**4h05min**).

Madeira wines

Local wines from the *tinta negra mole* grape are fortified with grape brandy, heated in an *estufa* at 40-45 °C for three months, then matured in oak in warm cellars for at least five years. Four types are produced:

• *Sercial*: a pale dry *(seco)* aperitif wine, served slightly chilled
• *Verdelho*: a tawny, medium dry *(meio seco)* wine, at its best with soup, cheese, cake or fruit
• *Bual*: a nutty, medium-sweet *(meio doce)* dessert or cheese wine
• *Malmsey (malvasia)*: a sweet *(doce)* after-dinner drink

When buying wine, ensure that the bottle bears the stamp of origin and quality issued by the Wine Institute of Madeira. We've often asked for a pre-prandial *sercial* — only to be offered a 'dry madeira' bearing no resemblance to the real thing!

Genuine madeiras can be sampled at the Madeira Wine Company (Av Arriaga 22), the Adegas de São Francisco (Av Arriaga 28 — next to the Tourist Office) for Blandy wines, and the Diogos Wine Shop (Av Arriaga 48) for Barbeito products.

Estreito: vine trellises over the Levada do Norte

Coral

You won't go hungry in Câmara de Lobos! There is a wide choice of bars and restaurants — after all, this is one of the island's main tourist attractions.

For many years our favourite has been Coral, by the church, with stunning views to Cabo Girão. It was first opened many years ago by a friend of ours who had trained at Reid's Hotel (and played for Marítimo!). At that time it was one of very few restaurants on the island with any 'style'.

But there's no point in illustrating it here. On our last visit it was being razed to the ground — to rise again in 2005 on a new esplanade with underground parking. Do stop by for a drink or snack — they are open all day — or for a really slap-up meal of freshly caught fish.

One of the house specialities — a combination of grilled parrotfish *(bodião)*, sea bream *(pargo)* and grouper *(garoupa)* — all of which they will fillet for you, if you like

CORAL
by the church (**942 469**
daily 10.00-24.00 €-€€

very wide menu, ranging from **soups**, **salads**, **omelettes** and **spaghetti** for a light meal

grilled fish is the speciality, especially the three-fish combination dish pictured above; also fish stew *(caldeirada)* and shellfish with rice *(arroz de mariscos)* for two; lobster thermidor; squid *(lulas)* on a skewer

meats include steaks, pork, chicken, *espetada*

good selection of **cakes** and **tarts**; Irish coffee

restaurants

eat

Tuna with onions
(atum cebolado)

Marinate the tuna in the other ingredients for 3-4 hours. Fry the fish (turning once) and onions together in olive oil until golden. Set aside and keep warm.

Reduce the marinade (minus the bay leaf) in the pan, then return the fish and onions to the sauce and simmer for a minute or two.

Fried cornmeal (milho frito)

Dissolve the flour in a bit of cold water. Bring all the other ingredients to the boil in 1.5 l water, then add the flour, stirring constantly until smooth and dry.

Spoon the mixture into *cold* shallow dishes and refrigerate, preferably over-night. Cut into cubes and fry in olive oil until golden. Drain on paper towels.

<u>Ingredients (for 4 people)</u>

for both recipes
salt to taste, olive oil for frying

for the fish
4 tuna steaks, washed
250 ml white wine
2 medium onions, sliced
4 cloves garlic, crushed
1 bay leaf

for the fried cornmeal
300 g white maize flour, sifted
1 tbsp lard *(sopa de banha)*
20 g shredded cabbage (sold in
   supermarkets on Maderia as
   'caldo verde' greens; at home
   use Chinese 'seaweed')
1 sprig fresh savoury

recipes

eat

This lovely ramble follows a narrow country road from Ponta do Pargo to Cabo and takes in a short stretch of the Levada Calheta–Ponta do Pargo. It's a favourite of ours — not only for the sea views, but because of the wonderful tea house/restaurant on the cliffs at Ponta do Pargo.

around ponta do pargo

WALK

Start the walk at the **church** in **Ponta do Pargo**. With the church on your left, walk left down the road signposted to Salão de Baixo, but turn right immediately, passing the **Casa do Povo**. *(Or, if you arrive at lunch time, first make for O Fio: keep straight down the Salão road to the cliffs. After lunch, return the same way but, just before the church, turn left.)* Ignore all paths off left. When you come to a crossing road (to the lighthouse), walk a few paces to the right uphill but, just before reaching the main ER101, go left downhill, passing a garage on the left with a tiled door frame. The road descends, crosses the **Ribeira dos Moinhos**, and rises into **Pedregal**, where you pass a **tap** on the right ('CMC'; **30min**).

Continue along the gently undulating road through flower-filled **Serrado** (notice the beautifully carved façade of a house on the right) and then

Distance: 10.5km/6.5mi; 4h

Grade: easy, with ascents/descents of 250m/820ft overall. *Note:* the levada may be dry outside summer.

Equipment: stout shoes, sunhat, warm clothing in cool weather, snacks, water

Transport: 🚌 80 or 142 (or 🚗) to Ponta do Pargo. Return on 🚌 80.

Refreshments: O Fio at the cliff-top viewpoint 1km below Ponta do Pargo (15min down, 20min back up)

Points of interest:
lighthouse at the most westerly point on the island
O Fio! (See page 121.)

Special note: There used to be a restaurant in Ponta do Pargo itself; it is now closed (except for private parties). The same owners now run O Fio in a far more beautiful setting, *but* it is impossible to do the whole walk *and* enjoy a meal if you are travelling by public transport. We would suggest first walking down to the restaurant, enjoying lunch, then heading back to the church to start the walk. End the walk on the EN 101 above Cabo, where bus 80 for Funchal passes at about 16.30. If you have time you can still explore a short way along the levada from there.

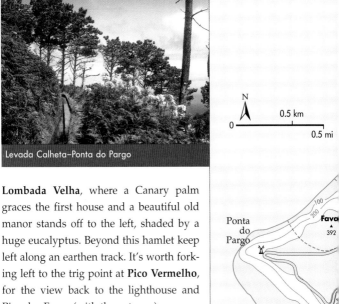

Levada Calheta–Ponta do Pargo

Lombada Velha, where a Canary palm graces the first house and a beautiful old manor stands off to the left, shaded by a huge eucalyptus. Beyond this hamlet keep left along an earthen track. It's worth forking left to the trig point at **Pico Vermelho**, for the view back to the lighthouse and Pico das Favas (with the antenna).

The track rises to a viewpoint and the chapel of **Nossa Senhora da Boa Morte** (**1h35min**). The chapel is unremarkable, but the grassy setting is idyllic — as the contented cows will agree! From the chapel follow the road uphill through **Cabo** to the ER101. Just *before* the main road, turn right on the **Levada Calheta–Ponta do Pargo** (a large water tank is on your left; **2h**). The levada crosses the main road in seven minutes (bus 80), then runs inland. Follow its meanderings

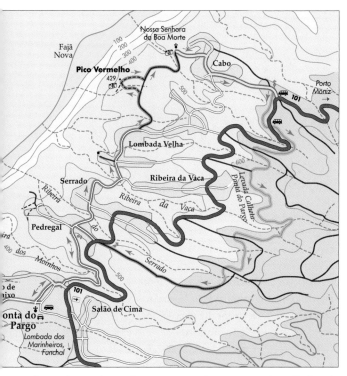

for under an hour. Four minutes after crossing the **Ribeira do Serrado** on a narrow levada 'bridge', turn right down an eroded jeep track (**3h**). Descend to the ER101 (by a **tap** on the right with a little garden), cross the road and continue straight down, back to the old road in **Pedregal**. Turn left; after 40m/yds you pass the **tap** encountered earlier. Retrace your steps to **Ponta do Pargo** (**4h**).

O Fio

On a rainy day there's nothing we like better than hopping on the morning bus and taking it all the way to Ponta do Pargo… just to enjoy our favourite meal. Then we can drink all the wine we like with lunch and nap on the bus back. But we've become so addicted to their *espada de vinho e alhos* that we even visit now on sunny days; no trip to Madeira is complete without this beautifully presented dish.

The photograph, taken from their garden, looks across to the viewpoint from where the old *fio* (goods hoist) lowered fruit and vegetables to ships bound for Funchal. Looking north from the viewpoint, you have the view shown opposite.

All the vegetables are really *fresh!* And the herbs for their special infusion are grown on pots around the terrace. In a nutshell: wonderful atmosphere, superb home cooking.

CASA DE CHÁ O FIO
Ponta do Pargo (882 170
open daily 10.30-21.00 €; credit cards are not accepted!

many different **omelettes** or **soups** for a light meal; **sandwiches**, including vegetarian

petiscos (various savouries) for two, or as an entrée)

fish *bacalhau*, octopus, shrimps, and their speciality — *espada de vinho e alhos* (see over)

meat dishes include pork stew with mushrooms, beef sauté *(picado)*, chicken giblets and gizzards *(moelas de galinha)*

specialities are teas (see over)

good **wine list**, but we were not impressed with the (expensive) local wine from Porto Moniz.

restaurants

eat

O FIO SPECIALITIES

Espada with wine and garlic (espada de vinho e alhos)

This recipe works well back home with any moist white *fleshy* fillets (allow 8 minutes cooking time per 2.5 cm thickness). At O Fio they use fresh tomatoes, but tinned will do.

Season the fillets with salt and pepper. Marinate with the wine, tomato, garlic, bay leaf, and oregano for an hour. Remove from the marinade, dry the fish, then dust with flour. Heat 1 cm of oil to smoking in a heavy-bottomed frying pan, then reduce the heat a little. Fry the fish, turning once (about 6-8min).

Ingredients (for 4 people)
8 fillets of *espada* (about
  750 g)
200 ml dry white wine
1 tin (400 g) chopped tomatoes
3 cloves garlic (crushed)
2 tbsp fresh oregano, chopped
  (or 1 tsp dried oegano
1 bay leaf
salt and pepper
flour to dust, olive oil to fry

Remove the fish, pat off the excess oil with paper towels, and set aside in a warm oven. Add the marinade to the olive oil, bring to the boil and simmer to reduce. Pour over the fish.

Serve as shown here! — with boiled potatoes, sweet potatoes (jacket-baked, then skin removed and sliced), salad, feijoada beans, onion rings, grated carrot and beetroot, lettuce and tomato.

recipes

eat

Bacalhau on sale in Funchal's market

Dried cod country style (bacalhau à moda do campo)

Dare you try your hand at *bacalhau*? These are the ingredients used at O Fio, which we've been successful with at home.

Soak the *bacalhau* in cold water for 24 hours, changing the water several times, then soak in milk for an hour. Place the fish in just enough fresh simmering water *(do not let it boil)* for about 15min, until tender. Carefully remove the skin and bones and flake into large pieces. Preheat the oven to 180°C, 350°F, gas mark 4.

Heat the olive oil in a heavy casserole, add the onions and cook until soft. Remove from heat; add the fish, potatoes, garlic and 1 tbsp of the coriander. Mix well.

Drizzle plenty of olive oil on top and bake, without a lid, until the top is golden — about 15min. To serve, sprinkle the rest of the fresh coriander on top.

Ingredients (for 4 people)

750 g *bacalhau* (dried salted cod; ask for centre cut or *lombo*)
500 g cooked sliced potatoes
2 medium onions, sliced
2 cloves garlic, crushed
250 ml olive oil
3 tbsp chopped fresh coriander

And for tea: marble cake, lemon cake and their special infusion: lemon balm, peppermint, lemon, fennel, anise and sugar cane. Other sweets on the menu include home-made mango mousse or iced-cream cake *(semifrio de bolacha)*

There's no need to take a coach tour to see the island. You can 'do your own thing'; it is far less expensive, and the buses plying tourist routes are of coach standard. Rodoeste offers this 'round the island' trip (better called 'round *half* the island!'); you can see the other half with bus 103 or 138.

'round the island'

EXCURSION

From Funchal the 09.00 bus travels the 'old road' (ER229) via **Câmara de Lobos** and **Estreito** (Walk 11). Notice the huge Sousa building materials depot on both sides of the road in **Campanário**: it spreads its tentacles further each year — testament to the frenzied building on the island. Soon the road curls steeply down into **Ribeira Brava** — there is a fine overview on the approach. You may have time to take a quick peek at the lovely church, founded in the 1500s.

From here you travel north through a great cleft splitting the island east/west. After a fairly straight run along a narrow canyon graced with poplars, the old road (ER228) begins its winding ascent in earnest. Beyond **Serra de Água**

Description: an all-day trip, beginning in Funchal and travelling north from Ribeira Brava, over Encumeada Pass to São Vicente. From there along the north coast to Porto Moniz (4-hour break) and back via the south coast.

Transport: Rodoeste 🚌 139 out; leaves Funchal at 09.00. Return from Porto Moniz on 🚌 80 at 16.00. *Tip: try to sit on the right-hand side of the bus for both journeys!* Information and tickets from the Rodoeste office at 50/52 Rua do Esmeraldo (near the Sugar Museum, 38 on the Funchal plan). (220 148. www.rodoeste.pt

Refreshments en route:
10min stop at Ribeira Brava
4h stop at Porto Moniz
10min stop at Calheta

Points of interest:
valleys south and north of Encumeada Pass
north coast, old north coast road
Porto Moniz and its lido
Ponta do Pargo
southwest coast, Calheta marina
splendid scenery throughout!

you pass several incredibly beautiful viewpoints on the right, towards the **high peaks**, and then the **Pousada dos Vinháticos** (see pages 105-107), beautifully sited below a ridge — the aptly named **Crista de Galo** ('Cock's Comb'). Further uphill is the Residencial

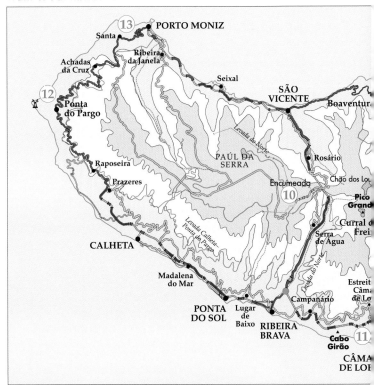

Encumeada, a very large hotel. The snaking ascent ends at **Encu-meada Pass**, just at the centre of the island (1004m/3293ft). Look up to the left for views of the high plateau, the **Paúl da Serra**. Opposite the little restaurant here at the pass are steps up to the magnificent Levada do Norte (Walk 10; photograph page 100).

Then the bus descends into São Vicente's welcoming valley,

MADEIRA

N

0 _____ 5 km
      3 mi

São
Jorge

SANTANA

Faial

Porto
da Cruz

PONTA DE SÃO
LOURENÇO

Pico do
Arieiro

Portela

Ribeiro
Frio

Caniçal

Santo
da Serra

MACHICO

Aeroporto

SANTA CRUZ

Monte

Camacha

FUNCHAL

⑦ walks in this book
⬤ expressway interchange

past **Chão dos Louros**, a lovely laurel grove on the right, with fireplaces. Soon you'll have good views over **Rosário**'s church and stream: in high summer the hayricks weave ribbons of gold into the tapestry of this emerald landscape. **São Vicente**, on the north coast, was one of the first villages on the island to be restored. In the 1980s the houses were repaired and painted in traditional Madeiran

Waterfall near São Vicente on the north coast road

colours, the pathways recobbled, and landscaping was carried out. Today the attractive old kernel of the village is hidden from passing traffic by a plethora of new buildings.

On leaving São Vicente, look out for the chapel built into a hollowed-out rock south of the bridge. Now the bus turns west along the north coast, passing the waterfall shown left. Much of the route now runs through tunnels, but the driver may take in parts of the one-way 'Antiga ER101'— the old corniche route, with more waterfalls and spectacular coastal views.

At **Seixal** the church perches high above the coast. Notice the steep vineyards here, edged with feathery heath-tree fencing to protect them from strong winds. Not far past Seixal, you should spot a palm-lined seaside promenade. Ahead lies **Ribeira da Janela**: the village takes its name from the 'window' *(janela)* in the 'sea-horse' rock just off the coast. Not far past a (perhaps still derelict) fish farm, you cross a bridge, pass a power station and go under a water pipe: this carries water from a very long levada in the bowels of the Paúl da Serra down to the power station.

Soon you're in **Porto Moniz**, where natural lava-rock pools have been beautifully incorporated into an extensive swimming complex with good facilities. You have time here for a four-hour break. We'd suggest that you *stay on* the bus up to Santa, then return via Walk 13 and have lunch — perhaps at the **Residencial Orca**, by the pools (see page 133).

Heading out of Porto Moniz the road climbs in steep hairpin bends, with magnificent views back over the village setting. Walk 13 begins 100m before the church in **Santa**. Further along, at **Achadas da Cruz**, there is a fantastic cable car (a 640m/2100ft descent), but unfortunately you won't see it from the main road.

The bus stops for 10 minutes at **Ponta do Pargo** but, alas, you won't be able to partake of the magnificent food at O Fio down on the cliffs. The next stretch of road follow the contours in and out of shady valleys, sometimes crossing the lovely Levada Calheta–Ponta do Pargo, shown on page 118.

Beyond **Raposeira** and **Prazeres**, the route makes for the coast again. At **Calheta** you descend past the church on the right (notice that it has been cut back to accommodate the road!) and then a power station. Coming onto the seafront promenade, there is a pretty viewpoint on the right and the restored remains of an old *aguardente* (sugar cane spirit) factory to the left. Calheta has a huge new marina. The restored cottages at the far end of **Madalena do Mar** are the most attractive part of this seaside village.

Some tunnels now take you to **Ponta do Sol**, with another church dating from the 15th century church and elegant façades facing the seaside promenade. **Lugar de Baixo** is reported to have the best climate on the island. The bus stops again for 10 minutes at **Ribeira Brava**; time to buy some fresh fruit and veg at the nearby fresh-air market. Retracing your outward route, the bus comes back into **Funchal** at about 8pm.

While road-building has ruined many of Madeira's old trails, several relatively short stretches still remain and have even been restored. Walks 3, 5, 8 and 9 all include sections of old cobbled trails. This descent to Porto Moniz, short as it is, offers magnificent views all the way down and intimate close-ups of country life.

to porto moniz

WALK

Start out on the main road in **Santa**, 100m/yds northeast of the church. Walk down the road signposted 'Caminho do Pico'. Go straight over a crossroads (**5min**) and, when the tar ends, continue down a *very steep* concrete lane, already enjoying the superb views shown left — over terraced fields and down to Porto Moniz and its offshore rock.

When the concrete lane ends (**20min**), take concrete steps off to the right: these quickly give way to the old zigzag trail — much easier on the knees. The trail eventually runs into a valley — a pleasant shady interlude, before descending near the ER101. It's worth taking the pretty cobbled path back to the right, up to the most southerly of the hairpin bends in the road … to make the walk last longer!

When you pass near the restaurant/viewpoint on the right (on the next hairpin bend), keep left downhill. Five minutes later, cross straight over a strip of concrete by some houses, on a narrower, steeper cobbled trail. Concrete steps take you down

Distance: 3km/2mi; 1h15min

Grade: moderate; a steep descent of 450m/1475ft. You must be sure-footed, but there is no danger of vertigo. *Virtually no shade*

Equipment: stout shoes (walking boots preferable), sunhat, water, walking stick, bathing things

Transport: 🚌 80 or 139 to Santa, or 🚗: park by the public WC, 100m northeast of the church. Return on 🚌 80 from Porto Moniz, back to base, or back to your car at Santa

Refreshents en route: bar/café in Santa and another at a viewpoint partway down the trail various restaurants, hotels, cafés and bars in Porto Moniz

Points of interest: views down to Porto Moniz old trail sea-water pools at Porto Moniz

The old trail to Porto Moniz

to a narrow levada not far above the **school** in **Porto Moniz**. Follow the levada to the right, then descend by road and steps (with street lights) to the **pool complex** (**1h15min**). The bus leaves from the roundabout just above the pools. The **Residencial Orca** is on the far side of the roundabout, but there is a very large choice of restaurants and café-bars in the village.

Residencial Orca

Perched just above the sea-water pools, for years the Orca was *the* place at Porto Moniz. It's certainly a pleasant place to spend the night; the sea-side rooms have huge terraces, where you can sunbathe or sit with a pre-prandial drink watching the endless breaking of the waves.

The Orca *does* cater for coach parties, but don't let this put you off. There is a veritable army of staff waiting to serve, and the coach guests (most of whom arrive just after 1pm) are seated in a different part of the dining room. In any case you can go in for for lunch as soon as bus 139 arrives (ahead of the coaches) or after you've finished Walk 13 (when they should have gone).

RESIDENCIAL ORCA
Porto Moniz (by the pools)
(850 000
Daily 12.00-15.30; 19.00-21.30 €-€€

large menu, with light and more substantial meals

entrées include 8 cold dishes, three soups, five omelettes

excellent **fish**, the usual *espada*, but with different fruits, *cherne* (stone bass), tuna with *milho frito*, parrotfish, grouper, sea bream, trout, salmon, sole, *bacalhau*

meats include beef, pork and lamb chops, roast chicken, beef with dates, *espetada* with *milho frito* and salad

Among the other hotels and restaurants at Porto Moniz is the **Residencial Salgueiro**, opposite the Orca on the far side of the roundabout (with a large souvenir shop below). It was being extended when we visited, so we had no opportunity to try it. They will open daily for lunch and dinner ((850 080). The Salgueiro shares a management team with the Estalagem Eira do Serrado, and we can hardly think of a better recommendation!

restaurants

eat

FISH SOUP AT ORCA

Fish soup *(sopa de peixe)*

Cut or tear the fish fillets into mouthful-sized chunks as shown in this photograph taken at Orca. (Make sure no bones remain.)

In a large heavy-bottomed saucepan, fry the onion and garlic lightly in the oil. Add the stock and bring to the boil. Turn down the heat, stir in the tomato purée, then add the potatoes. Cook just below boiling for 6 minutes, then add the carrots and peppers and cook for another 6 minutes.

Ingredients (for 4 people)

300 g *espada* fillet (or other fairly solid fish)
2 potatoes, in large cubes
1 small onion, finely chopped
handful of finely-sliced carrots
2 tbsp finely-diced red peppers
1.5 l vegetable stock
two tbsp tomato purée
spices to taste: crushed garlic, bay leaf, clove, allspice, parsley
1 tbsp wine vinegar
20 ml olive oil

Remove half of the potatoes and whizz with a little stock; set aside. Add the fish, vinegar and spices to the soup and continue cooking for about 4 minutes (until the fish is cooked, but still in solid pieces). Then stir the puréed potatoes back into the soup to thichen.

This soup is especially good served with *pão da casa* (see page 92), which is often drizzled with olive oil rather than spread with butter.

recipes

eat

Transport: bus operators and web sites

Only journey times and some last return buses are shown. See the operator's web site (**H**: www.horariosdofunchal.pt **R**: www.rodoeste.pt) for full timetables and pages 12-13 for details of *printed* timetables. Departure points for all buses are shown on the plan inside the front cover.

Excursion 1: frequent town buses to return. **H**

Walk 1: frequent town buses for access and return. **H**

Walk 2: frequent town buses for access and return. **H**

Walk 3: journey time for bus 81 is about 45min. If you want to stay for *dinner,* the last buses are at 20.30 and 21.30+. **H**

Walk 4: journey time for bus 29 or 77 about 45min to Camacha, 1h from Santo da Serra (bus 77). Last 77 return bus 18.00 or 20.30+. **H**

Walk 5: best outgoing bus is 56; journey time about 50min; only suitable return is bus 103 at 18.35. **H**

Walk 6: bus 113 at 08.30*, 09.00, 11.15*, 12.15; returns 14.00, 17.00, 18.00, 19.00•, 19.40*, 21.00=•; journey time 1h10min. **No web site**

Walk 7: bus 53 or 78 journey time 1h15min; last bus from Portela at 18.50+ (bus 53). **H**

Walk 8: bus 56 or 103 journey time to Santana 2h10min; last return from Arco de São Jorge bus 103 at 16.30. **H**

Walk 9: bus 6 journey time 3h10min to Boaventura; 4h to Arco. Returns up till 17.50 from Arco; 18.05 from Boaventura. **R** Also bus 103 from Arco at 16.30. **H**

Walk 10: bus 6 (07.45) or 139 (09.00); journey time 2h; bus 6 at 16.00 to return. **R**

Walk 11: frequent 96 buses to go and many coastal return buses. **R**

Walk 12: bus 80 a much faster service (2h20min) than 142 (4h), but 142 arrives at noon and 80 at 12.20. Last return bus (80) at 16.50. **R**

Walk 13: as Excursion 2, page 125, or bus 80; journey time 3h. **R**

+Mon-Fri only; =Sat only; *not Sun; •Sun only

We've been visiting Madeira for many years, doing what we like most — walking, eating and enjoying the Portuguese wines. Only in the last decade have excellent restaurants opened all over the island; in the past good food was limited to Funchal and just a few countryside establishments that still exist and are mentioned in this book.

About ten years ago John was diagnosed coeliac and, more recently, lactose intolerant. Food intolerances are becoming ever more common, and we know *there are a lot of you out there!* Even if you have learned to cope at home, it can be very daunting to go on holiday. *Will the food in restaurants be safe? Will I be able to buy gluten- and dairy-free foods?*

If you suffer from food intolerance you have probably already learned at home that what initially seems a penance in fact becomes a challenge and eventually a joy. We eat far healthier meals now than we did before, with fewer additives. Nowhere is this more enjoyable than around the Mediterranean and on Madeira, where olive oil, fish, tomatoes and 'alternative' grains and flours are basic to the diet. Many, many dishes are *naturally* gluten- and dairy-free.

Of course food intolerances *are* restrictive — in the sense that we have to carry, buy or bake gluten-free breads and sweets, and we always need access to dairy-free 'milk', 'cream', 'yoghurt' and 'butter'. So over the years we've sussed out eating gf, df on the island, and it's *so simple.*

EAT GF, DF

EATING IN RESTAURANTS

The most common **first courses** are soup, fish and salads. Soups are *not* thickened with flour and very few contain cream — even though they look and taste 'creamy'. The secret is that they are thickened with a potato or vegetable (often pumpkin) purée.

The most popular **main courses** are grilled fish, steaks and chops. Sauces *(molhos)* usually consist of wine, tomatoes, onions, herbs and garlic, all reduced. If you are a sauce addict, like John, it is safer to *ask* (see inside back flap for help in Portuguese, although the staff usually speak English); you are likely to be pleasantly surprised. *Fried* fish is invariably dusted with flour (otherwise it is more difficult to cook), but just *ask:* they are happy to do it for you without flour — or take your own flour with you. All the restaurants recommended here cook meals individually; the staff are always accessible. For instance, our super-favourite fish meal, at O Fio, illustrated on page 122, was fried *without* flour (but still retained its shape).

We are always too full to have **dessert** but, if you have a sweet tooth, make for the restaurants on pages 42-43; the chestnut cake is 100% gf, df and out of this world. All restaurants offer fruit (including many exotic fruits) for dessert, and some have gf, df chocolate dishes (made with dark chocolate); *ask!*

SELF-CATERING

While many hotels on the island cater for food intolerances, we discovered the joy of self-catering years ago. What a liberation! Room to swing a cat (or, more likely, chop up a rabbit). Tables where you can spread out your maps and bus timetables. Sofas to loll about on with a good book on a rainy day.

But if we're staying in self-catering for a couple of weeks or more, we *do* treat ourselves to the odd night at one of the beautifully-sited hotels mentioned in this book. It's relatively easy to cope for just a night or two, even if they don't have the supplies. They will let you use their fridges (just take a carrier bag or container and label with your name and room number); the non-perishables can stay in your room.

Gf, df shopping

Madeiran supermarkets have no selection of gluten- or dairy-free products, except for the *naturally* gf flour used on the island, corn meal *(farinha de milho)* and a fair selection of soya sweets. There are three main **health food** shops in Funchal, each of which caters for food intolerances (and vegetarians).

Bioforma at 31 Rua Queimada de Cima, ☏ 229 262 (39 on the plan) has a wide range, all kept on the lower ground floor, where there is also a small **vegetarian deli**. While they usually have imported **gf bread** on the shelves, in the freezer they stock a gf loaf made on the island (ask for it at the deli counter). There is also a good selection of breakfast cereals, biscuits, pastas (Glutano seems to have conquered the market on the island for the moment, but there are other brands of which we had never heard — a good opportunity to sample). You *can* buy your bread and biscuits here, but better still, buy some direct from the bakery, a stone's throw away (see panel opposite).

For **lactose intolerants** there is **rice milk** and a wealth of **soya** products — milk, juices, sweets, and the essential 'cream' for pouring and cooking (both Provamel and a Portuguese brand called 'Soyacrem').

Usually they also stock a 100% vegetable spread based on sunflower oil (ask at the deli counter), but we recently spent a month on the island unable to buy any dairy-free spread (and were amazed at how easy it was to do without!). *Do not fall for* 'Planta', a spread available in all supermarkets which claims to be *'100% vegetal'*, but in fact contains whey!

There is a second **Bioforma** at 31 Rua dos Netos, but it has less stock and we found it not worth the trip.

Bio-Logos at 34 Rua Nova de S Pedro, ℓ 236 868 (40 on the plan) is also very well stocked with most of the items listed under Bioforma. It also specialises in **vegetarian food**, with a pleasant **vegetarian café-restaurant**.

FABRICA DE STO ANTONIO
Travessa do Forno 27-29
(on the corner of 5 Outubro; 16 on the plan) ℓ 220 255

This wonderful old bakery (founded in 1893) makes fresh gf bread on Thursdays and Fridays (but there is always some in stock). Their main customer for gf is the Savoy Hotel. You could phone and order in advance; when you collect it, buy some gf biscuits as well (a large selection in stock). The bread keeps well out of the fridge and is very good toasted or *untoasted*. Contains rice and tapioca flour, corn and potato starch, egg whites, corn gum, oil, yeast, sugar, salt and vinegar.

Gf, df cooking

We've made all the **recipes** in this book using gluten- and dairy-free ingredients. Basically we just used a 1:1 substitution, and the cooking method was unchanged.

One of the recipes ('Reid's Cake', see pages 36-37) was in fact originally a gluten- and dairy-free recipe from Dietary Specials (www.nutritionpoint.co.uk). If you make it using normal wheat flour, we can only hope it tastes as good!

The only problem we have is with *frying,* when the recipe calls for a mixture of oil and butter (or just butter). Most 100% vegetable spreads spit all over the place because they contain so much water. Check the ingredients: the best spreads contain 60% sunflower oil, some palm and perhaps coconut oil; water *should rank no higher than third* on the list of ingredients. Note, too, that lard *(sopa de banha)* is widely available on the island.

CONVERSION TABLES

Weights		Volume		Oven temperatures		
						gas
10 g	1/2 oz	15 ml	1 tbsp	°C	°F	mark
25 g	1 oz	55 ml	2 fl oz	140°C	275°F	1
50 g	2 oz	75 ml	3 flz oz	150°C	300°F	2
110 g	4 oz	150 ml	1/4 pt	170°C	325°F	3
200 g	7 oz	275 ml	1/2 pt	180°C	350°F	4
350 g	12 oz	570 ml	1 pt	190°C	375°F	5
450 g	1 lb	1 l	1-3/4 pt	200°C	400°F	6
700 g	1 lb 8 oz	1.5 l	2-1/2 pt	220°C	425°F	7
900 g	2 lb			230°C	430°F	8
1.35 g	3 lb			240°C	475°F	9

MENU ITEMS

abacate avocado
abóbora marrow, pumpkin
açorda bread soup with garlic
água water
  com gás sparkling
  sem gas still
aguardente sugar cane spirit
alcaparras capers
alecrim rosemary
alface lettuce
alho garlic
amêijoas cockles
amêndoa almond
ananás pineapple
arroz rice
  de mariscos rice with shellfish
assado(a) roast
atum tuna
aziete olive oil
azeitonas olives
bacalhau dried salted cod
batata potato
  doce sweet potato
bife beef (or steak, as in *bife de atum* — tuna steak)
filete fillet
lombo sirloin
bodião parrotfish
bolo cake

do caco flat bread
do mel molasses cake
borrego lamb
bravo(a) wild
cabrito baby goat
calamares squid
caldeirada stew (usually fish)
camarão shrimp, prawns
caril curry
carne meat (usually pork)
caseiro(a) home-made
castanha chestnut
cebola onion
cerveja beer
chá tea
cherne stone bass
chouriço spicy pork sausage
coelho rabbit
cogumelos mush-rooms
corvina a local fish
costeleta cutlet
cozido(a) boiled (also: meat and vegetable stew)
do dia daily special
dose portion
dourada dory
enguia eel
ervas herbs

espada a local fish
espadarte swordfish
esparguete spaghetti
espetada beef cubes on a skewer
  em pau de louro on a laurel stick
faisão pheasant
farinha (wheat) flour
fatia slice
favas broad beans
feijoada stew with (haricot) beans
fiambre cooked ham
fígado liver
frango chicken
frito(a) fried
funcho fennel
galinha hen
gambas giant prawns
garoupa grouper
gelado ice cream
grelhado(a) grilled
lagosta lobster
langostins crayfish
lapas limpets
legumes vegetables
leitão suckling pig
leite milk
lentilhas lentils
limão lemon
lingua tongue

linguado sole
lombo loin, sirloin
louro bay (laurel)
lulas squid
maça apple
maionese mayon-naise
manga mango
manteiga butter
  de alho garlic butter
maracujá passion fruit
marisco shellfish
massa pasta (or pastry casing)
mel honey
melão melon
mexilhões mussels
milho cornmeal
  frito fried
mista/mistura mixed
molho sauce
manjerona majoram
mostarda mustard
natas cream
nozes nuts
oregão oregano
ovo egg
pão bread
pargo sea bream
pastel small tart
pepino cucumber
peixe fish

picado, picadinho
   sautéed meat
picante hot
peru turkey
pimenta pepper
   (spice)
pimento pepper
   (vegetable)
piri-piri hot red
   pepper sauce
polvo octopus
porco pork
presunto smoked
   ham
pudim crème
   caramel
quiejo cheese
 da serra fresh
   mountain cheese
quente hot (as in
   warm, not spicy)
recheado(a) stuffed
salmão salmon
salsa parsley
sande sandwich
sardinhas sardines
semilha potato
sidra cider
sopa soup
sumo juice
tarte tarte, pie
tomilho thyme
tosta toast(ed)
   sandwich
toucinho bacon
trigo wheat
truta trout
vaca cow
vinho wine (see
   pages 8, 113)
vitela veal

SHOPPING TERMS

apple *maçã*
avocado *abacate*
bacon *toucinho*
bay leaves *louro em folhas*
beans *feijão*
beef* *bife*
beer *cerveja*
bread *pão*
broad beans *favas*
butter *manteiga*
cabbage *couve*
cake *bolo*
carrot *cenoura*
cheese *queijo*
cherries *cerejas*
chestnut *castanha*
chicken *frango*
cider *sidra*
cockles *amêijoas*
cod, dried *bacalhau*
coffee *café*
cornmeal *milho*
crayfish *langostins*
cream *natas*
cucumber *pepino*
dates *tâmaras*
eel *enguia*
eggs *ovos*
fennel *funcho*
fish *peixe* (many are
   unfamiliar; see
   'Menu items'
   above)
flour *farinha*; maize
   flour *milho*
fruit *fruta*
garlic *alho*
grapes *uvas*

ham, cooked
   fiambre; smoked
   presunto
herbs *ervas*
ice cream *gelado*
juice *sumo*
lamb* *borrego*
lard *sopa de banha*
lemon *limão*
lettuce *alface*
limpets *lapas*
liver *fígado*
lobster *lagosta*
mango *manga*
marjoram *manje-rona*
marrow, pumpkin
   abóbora
melon *melão*
milk *leite*
mushrooms *cogu-melos*
mussels *mexilhões*
mustard *mostarda*
nuts *nozes*
octopus *polvo*
olive oil *aziete*
olives *azeitonas*
onion *cebola*
orange *laranja*
parsley *salsa*
pear *pêra*
peas *ervilhas*
pepper *pimenta*
pig, suckling *leitão*
pineapple *ananás*
pork* *(carne de) porco*
potatoes *batatas, semilhas*; sweet
   batatas doces

prawns *camarão*
   giant *gambas*
passion fruit
   maracujá
rabbit *coelho*
rice *arroz*
rosemary *alecrim*
salmon *salmão*
salt *sal*
sardines *sardinhas*
sausage, spicy
   chouriço
sole *linguado*
soup *sopa*
spinach *espinafre*
spices, condiments
   condimentos
squid *calamares*
sugar *açucar*
swordfish *espadarte*
tea *chá*
thyme *tomilho*
tomato *tomate*
tongue *lingua*
   beef *de vaca*
trout *truta*
tuna *atum*
turkey *peru*
veal *vitela*
vegetables *legumes*
vinegar *vinagre*
wine *vinho*
water *água*
   plain *sem gás*
   sparkling *com gás*

*cuts of meat
cutlet, chop
   costeleta
loin, sirloin *lombo*
filet *filete*

bold type: photograph; *italic type:* map

INDEX

First edition © 2005
Published by Sunflower Books
PO Box 36061, London SW7 3WS
www.sunflowerbooks.co.uk

ISBN 1-85691-277-9

Cover photograph: landslip (fajã) below Cabo Girão (Walk 11)

Photographs: John Underwood
Maps: John Underwood, adapted from Portuguese IGC and military maps
Series design: Jocelyn Lucas
Cookery editor: Marina Bayliss
A CIP catalogue record for this book is available from the British Library.
Printed and bound in Spain by Grafo Industrias Gráficas, Basauri

Before you go ...
log on to
www.sunflowerbooks.co.uk
and click on '**updates**', to see if we have been notified of any changes to
the routes or restaurants.

When you return ...
do let us know if any routes have changed because of road-building, storm
damage or the like. Have any of our restaurants closed — or any new ones
opened on the route of the walk? (Not Funchal restaurants, please; these
books are not intended to be complete restaurant guides!)
Send your comments to mail@sunflowerbooks.co.uk